THE OXFORD
HISTORY
OF
BRITAIN

VOLUME IV

THE OXFORD
HISTORY OF BRITAIN

This five-volume series, edited by Kenneth O. Morgan, is the work of ten historians who are all distinguished authorities in their fields.

VOLUME I. ROMAN AND ANGLO-SAXON BRITAIN
 PETER SALWAY, The Open University. *Roman Britain*
 JOHN BLAIR, The Queen's College, Oxford. *The Anglo-Saxons*

VOLUME II. THE MIDDLE AGES
 JOHN GILLINGHAM, London School of Economics and Political Science. *The Early Middle Ages*
 RALPH A. GRIFFITHS, University College of Swansea. *The Later Middle Ages*

VOLUME III. THE TUDORS AND STUARTS
 JOHN GUY, University of St Andrews. *The Tudor Age*
 JOHN MORRILL, Selwyn College, Cambridge. *The Stuarts*

VOLUME IV. THE EIGHTEENTH CENTURY AND THE AGE OF INDUSTRY
 PAUL LANGFORD, Lincoln College, Oxford. *The Eighteenth Century*
 CHRISTOPHER HARVIE, University of Tübingen. *Revolution and the Rule of Law*

VOLUME V. THE MODERN AGE
 H. C. G. MATTHEW, St Hugh's College, Oxford. *The Liberal Age*
 KENNETH O. MORGAN, University College of Wales, Aberystwyth. *The Twentieth Century*

THE OXFORD
HISTORY
OF
BRITAIN

EDITED BY
KENNETH O. MORGAN

VOLUME IV
THE EIGHTEENTH CENTURY AND
THE AGE OF INDUSTRY

Paul Langford and Christopher Harvie

Oxford   New York
OXFORD UNIVERSITY PRESS
1992

Oxford University Press, Walton Street, Oxford OX2 6DP

Oxford New York Toronto
Delhi Bombay Calcutta Madras Karachi
Petaling Jaya Singapore Hong Kong Tokyo
Nairobi Dar es Salaam Cape Town
Melbourne Auckland

and associated companies in
Berlin Ibadan

Oxford is a trade mark of Oxford University Press

The text of this edition first published 1984
in The Oxford Illustrated History of Britain
Revised text first published by Oxford University Press in five volumes 1992

British Library Cataloguing in Publication Data
Data available
ISBN 0–19–285266–3

Library of Congress Cataloging in Publication Data
The Oxford history of Britain / edited by Kenneth O. Morgan.
p.   cm.
Text based on: The Oxford illustrated history of Britain.
Includes bibliographical references.
Contents: v. 4. The eighteenth century and the age of industry / Paul Langford and
Christopher Harvie
1. Great Britain—History.   I. Morgan, Kenneth O.   II. Oxford
illustrated history of Britain.
941—dc20   DA30.093 1992   92–1156
ISBN 0–19–285266–3

Printed in Great Britain by
Biddles Ltd.
Guildford and King's Lynn

CONTENTS

LIST OF MAPS

The maps on pp. 30 and 31 are based on two in *Transport and Economy: The Turnpike Roads of Eighteenth-Century Britain*, by Eric Pawson, by kind permission of Academic Press, Inc. (London) Ltd.

1. *The Eighteenth Century*

(1688–1789)

PAUL LANGFORD

Revolution and its Repercussions

THE historical importance of the Revolution of 1688—the 'Glorious Revolution'—has inevitably fluctuated in the process of constant reinterpretation by successive generations. It has fared particularly badly at the hands of the twentieth century, and threatens to disappear altogether under the demands of modern historical scholarship. The decisive triumph of the liberal and democratic spirit, beloved of Macaulay and the Victorian Whigs, has dwindled into the conservative reaction of a selfish oligarchy. Especially when compared with modern revolutions, it seems rather to resemble a palace coup than a genuine shift of social or political power. This impression is reinforced, perhaps, by what was seen at the time as one of its most creditable features—the relative absence of physical violence. Yet this aspect can be exaggerated. In Scotland, the supporters of the deposed king had to be crushed by force of arms, a process which was completed in 1689. In Ireland there was positively a blood-bath, one which still holds a prominent place in Irish myths and memories. When the siege of Londonderry was lifted, and James II decisively defeated at the battle of the Boyne, Ulster Protestants certainly considered their salvation to be glorious, but they can hardly have thought of it as bloodless.

The story might easily have been the same in England. The

former royalist Nicholas L'Estrange testified that only chance, the disarray of James II's friends, and above all the king's surprising failure to raise the royal standard in his own realm, prevented a civil war as ferocious as those of the mid-century. Yet L'Estrange's very relief that his family had been saved further sacrifices in the cause of the Stuarts perhaps provides a clue to the comparative tranquillity associated with the making of the revolution in England. A perceptible sense of compromise, of the need to step back from the brink, carries over the centuries from the debates of the assembly which met in London in January 1689. The Convention, which transformed itself into Parliament by the simple expedient of passing an Act to that effect, displayed an understandable desire to legitimize what was manifestly illegitimate by following as far as possible the procedural forms employed at the Restoration in 1660. On matters of substance, the priority was plainly to find a common core of agreement rather than to test the more extreme solutions offered by either side. William of Orange was made king, with Mary as queen. Tories, led by Danby, would have preferred Mary as sole monarch, or some species of regency ruling technically in the name of James II. But the Protestant saviour would accept nothing less than the crown, and so it was. None the less, every effort was made to conceal the revolutionary nature of what was being done. Though James's supposedly illegal acts—particularly his reliance on a standing army and his recourse to the dispensing and suspending powers—were formally condemned, the Bill of Rights went out of its way to pretend that the deposed king had in effect abdicated, leaving a deserted realm no alternative but to seek the protection of the House of Orange. Implausible though this appeared, it was sufficient to secure the assent of a majority of the ruling class. There were, inevitably, exceptions. Some churchmen, led by Sancroft, the Archbishop of Canterbury, and two of the bishops who had helped bring James II down in the Seven Bishops Case, declined to take even the cautiously worded oaths designed by the Convention. Others, like the Nottingham

Tories, old champions of the court in the reaction of 1681–7, wrestled with the concept of a rightful king who owed his title to a *de facto* decision of Parliament, but not to the *de jure* ordinance of heaven.

Yet the substantive acceptance of parliamentary monarchy was achieved. The profound importance of this achievement was obscured not merely by conscious attempts to avoid dogmatic prescriptions in 1689 but by the long agonies which followed. Passive obedience and non-resistance continued to be influential concepts, buttressed as they were by elaborate arguments stressing the providential nature of the Protestant Wind in 1688, and the duty of every citizen to co-operate with any form of authority rather than submit to anarchy. For a generation, these notions continued to work on men's minds, bestowing a sense of legitimacy on the rage and despair felt by many who had seen the necessity for what had happened in 1688 but found it difficult to live with all the consequences. Beyond that, they sank into the Anglican orthodoxy of the eighteenth-century mind and helped secure the underlying authoritarianism which was to remain an important element of political ideology in the age of the American and French Revolutions. But, with this reservation, the major change of course carried out in 1688 can be seen to have been truly revolutionary. The Bill of Rights clearly overrode the hereditary right which formed the basis of the restored constitution of 1660 and replaced it with the will of the nation expressed through Parliament. First William and Mary, then Mary's sister Anne, and finally, after the death of the latter's son the duke of Gloucester in 1700, the Electors of Hanover (descended from James I through the female line) all owed their title to the determination of the propertied classes. At a time when absolutism, both in theory and practice, seemed to be in the ascendant in the Western world, the importance of this transformation should not be underestimated. Eighteenth- and nineteenth-century Whigs exaggerated the coherence and completeness of the contract theory which seemed to have triumphed in 1689 and they underrated the tensions, contradictions, and conflicts which it entailed. But they were fundamentally correct in seeing it as a historic turning-point involving the decisive rejection of an entire conception of government.

The status of the monarchy was very much the conscious concern of the revolutionaries of 1688. It is doubtful whether many of them foresaw the consequences of their actions in terms of England's relations with foreign powers. In this respect, indeed, the importance of the Revolution is undenied and undeniable. Before 1688, the policy of successive rulers, Cromwell, Charles II, and James II, had been largely pro-French and anti-Dutch. After 1688 France was to become a more or less permanent enemy, and certainly a constant rival in the battle for supremacy overseas. The scale of conflict was also novel. The Nine Years War (1688–97) and the War of Spanish Succession (1702–13) involved Britain in both Continental and colonial warfare as she had not been involved since the Elizabethan struggle with Spain, and in the interim the technological and strategic complexity of war-making had vastly increased. The part of Englishmen in this unexpected, if not unpredictable, consequence of the Revolution was affected by various considerations. In terms of grand strategy, the priority was to combat Louis XIV's expansionist policies in the Low Countries, and to prevent the erection of a mighty new Bourbon empire comprising the Spanish as well as French monarchy. The interests of commerce, which once had required protection against Dutch economic enterprise, could now be said to dictate an aggressive stance towards the more sustained challenge of French competition, and especially the assertion of Britain's right to a share in the trade if not the territory of the Spanish empire. These arguments were woven by the Whigs into a systematic case for an interventionist foreign policy, expressed most clearly in the Continental campaigns of William III and Marlborough. But such considerations would not have led many Englishmen to approve the formidable outlay of expenditure and resources in these years if it had not been for the dynastic issue. The Nine

Years War has appropriately been called the War of the English Succession. William would hardly have set sail for Torbay in 1688 if he had not assumed that the English alliance against France would follow logically from his own intervention in English affairs. Yet in fact diplomatic and military support from his new subjects was made much more likely by Louis XIV's imprudent championship of James II. French backing for the Jacobite camp was withdrawn when an uneasy peace was negotiated in 1697. But four years later, with the Spanish Succession at stake, and Europe on the verge of war once more, it was again Louis's support for the Stuarts, this time in the shape of James's son the Old Pretender, which convinced many reluctant Englishmen of the case for involvement in a Continental conflict.

One of the most startling aspects of the wars was the sheer success of English arms, particularly under Marlborough in the War of Spanish Succession. It was not just that the Protestant Succession was effectively secured at least for the present. More striking still was the new reputation earned by a country widely regarded as little more than a pensioner of France only a short time before. Marlborough's triumphs at Blenheim and Ramillies, not to say Rooke's at Gibraltar and Stanhope's at Minorca, established Britain as a major force in Continental politics, a substantial power in the Mediterranean, and a worthy competitor for France overseas. The latter stages of the war, in which military progress seemed to diminish in direct proportion to national expenditure, removed the loftier ambitions suggested by the dazzling victories of the Blenheim period, but when peace was made at Utrecht in 1713 sufficient was secured to retain the essential impact of the successes, and even to create the impression of what French diplomatic historians have termed the 'English hegemony' in Europe.

Hardly less important was the domestic impact of warfare. The cost of the wars amounted to almost £150 million in an age when peacetime expenditure was thought excessive at two millions per annum. This vast outlay required a corresponding rise in levels of taxation, with widespread political repercussions. But more interesting in retrospect is the fact that a large proportion of the bill, approximately one-third, was met by borrowing. Sums of this order could only be found in a buoyant and flexible money market, such as that created by the economic conditions of the late seventeenth century. Though land values were seriously affected by agrarian recession, trade had enjoyed a great upsurge in the 1680s and the investment surpluses released were to wash over the economy for a good many years. A post-revolution government, sorely in need of cash and prepared to mortgage the incomes of unborn generations of taxpayers to permit a competitive interest rate, offered promising investment possibilities. The financiers whose initiative eventually led to the foundation of the Bank of England in 1694 were not, in principle, engaging in anything new. As long as wars had been undertaken, governments had been forced to rely on loans from the business community. What was new was the political infrastructure which was necessitated by the exceptionally heavy borrowing of this period. The credit-worthiness of the new regime, based as it was on a parliamentary title, was negligible without the clear understanding that the propertied classes would ultimately be prepared to foot the bill. Without a matching recognition on the part of the regime that it must closely collaborate with those classes and their representatives, no such understanding could exist. The National Debt and all it entailed was built on this essential nexus of interest linking an illegitimate dynasty, the financial world, and the taxpaying public.

As war followed war and decade followed decade the burden of debt grew. Successive governments found it ever harder to avoid borrowing, and the main function of those taxes which were raised was often merely to pay the interest charges on the debt. With hindsight, the advantages of this system, without precise parallel in contemporary Europe, are obvious. The political security of an otherwise somewhat shaky regime was much enhanced, and national resources in wartime much boosted by this machinery for channelling private wealth into public expenditure. At the time, the disadvantages attracted more attention. The pretence that the National Debt could actually be repaid and the nation released from the threat of bankruptcy became increasingly thin. The anxieties of a society traditionally ill-disposed to taxation in general and new forms of taxation in particular made the task of the Treasury and the Committee of Ways and Means increasingly harrowing. Yet, even at the time, there were those who had a shrewd perception of one quite priceless political advantage of the new system. This arose from its impact on Parliament, and especially on the House of Commons. For everything depended on Parliament's part in this elaborate process, and Parliament was understandably jealous of its rights in matters of finance. The land tax, the basic guarantee of the taxpayer's commitment to the National Debt, was cautiously voted for a year at a time. Even the customs and excise duties, granted for much longer periods, were extended and renewed only after the most prolonged debate and haggling. The 'budget' was nominally an achievement of the mid-century, when the term was first used during Henry Pelham's time as First Lord of the Treasury (1743–54). But its essential features can be traced back to the Revolution, and it is this aspect of 1689 which more than anything else finally secured Parliament's central place in constitutional development. At times in the seventeenth century it had been possible to see the legislature as a faintly absurd and decidedly irritating survival of England's medieval past, an irrational obstruction to efficient monarchical government which might profitably be dispensed with altogether. Now its future was secure; since 1689 Parliament has met for a substantial period every year. In this sense the Revolution gave a novel twist to an old problem: eighteenth-century politicians asked themselves not how to do away with the need for Parliament, or even how to crush it. Rather they had to consider how to manipulate it. The arts of management were to provide the key to the conduct of Georgian politics.

It was impossible in the late seventeenth century to engage in political revolution without raising the prospect or the spectre (depending on one's viewpoint) of ecclesiastical revolution. In this respect the Revolution of 1688 was perhaps important not merely for what it did but for what it failed to do. Many contemporaries hoped for a radical revision of the Church settlement of the 1660s. There was talk of a truly comprehensive national Church, and for some Dissenters, particularly the Presbyterians, the possibilities of reconcilation to the establishment seemed stronger than at any time since Hampton Court in 1604. In the event, however, their hopes were dashed. As in 1662, the Anglican squirearchy would permit no weakening of the hierarchical and episcopalian structure of the Church. It would be inappropriate to talk of a Laudian or high-church reaction at this time. But any sign of genuine *rapprochement* with the Dissenters was quickly extinguished. Instead, the latter were offered the least that could be offered against the background of recent events, a grudging toleration. The Toleration Act of 1689 in effect granted freedom of worship to Protestant nonconformists in premises licensed by Anglican bishops, provided that those concerned shared the basic doctrines laid down in the Thirty-nine Articles and sanctioned by the Act of Uniformity. This seemed a far cry from the prospect held out to Dissenters of all kinds by James II.

No doubt for this reason, it has been customary to play down the full significance of the Toleration Act. An extremely qualified liberty permitted to those whose beliefs were defined in strictly qualified terms seemed a poor reward for men who had resisted the temptations offered by the Declarations of Indulgence and had welcomed William of Orange. But such judgements depend heavily on the point of view. For Dissenters who had been vigorously persecuted as recently as the early 1680s, the Toleration Act provided an unprecedented statutory security. From the vantage point of anxious churchmen it was no less important to maintain the substance of the Restoration Settlement. The Prayer Book of 1662 was to remain the liturgical basis of Anglican worship until the twentieth century; but in 1689 it seemed to offer a precarious platform of doctrine without which established Protestantism might be lost. Paradoxically, the resulting exclusiveness of the Church had much to do with England's eighteenth-century reputation as a civilized society in a barbarous world. A comprehensive national Church embracing all but a small number of sectaries and papists would have been a very different matter from a restricted religious establishment, co-existing with large numbers of nonconformists. The difference was perhaps a tolerant, pluralist society. The legal recognition of liberty of worship went far beyond what had been achieved in most of Europe, and Voltaire was to hold it up as the crucial element in the development of a free society. If so, it was to a large extent the consequence of the Revolution.

The achievements of these years had a price in the social tensions and political conflicts which marked the Augustan era. Pre-eminent among the signs of strain was indeed the plight of the religious establishment. The great cry of the period was 'The Church in Danger'. Whether it was truly in danger seems doubtful in retrospect. Toleration was obviously a fearful blow to those who dreamed of reviving a Laudian church. But the swelling tide of latitudinarian theology and sentiment made it seem innocuous enough to most. Moreover, the political monopoly enjoyed by Anglicans under the Test and Corporation Acts was left intact by the Revolution Settlement. Here, however, was the rub. For in practice there was every indication that Dissenters were able to challenge and evade this monopoly. The readiness of many nonconformists to resort to occasional conformity, annually taking the sacraments according to the Anglican rite in order to meet the requirements of the statutes, and for the rest worshipping in their own meeting houses, was a constant source of irritation to their enemies. Whether the actual practice of occasional conformity grew in this period is uncertain. But it was unquestionably more noticeable now that Dissenting chapels were publicly recognized, and now that the double standard apparently observed by those who attended them was plain to all. Moreover, the general climate of the 1690s and 1700s provoked anxiety and even hysteria on the part of churchmen. Theological speculation and deistic tendencies were much discussed and much feared. John Toland's *Christianity Not Mysterious*, one of the earliest and most systematic attempts to popularize the case for 'natural' against 'revealed' religion, began a torrent of polemical debate on such matters in 1697. Nor did it help that some of the worst offenders were themselves clergy of the established Church. Samuel Clarke, the Whig sceptic whose assault on Trinitarianism brought the wrath of Convocation upon his head in 1712, and Benjamin Hoadly, who held three bishoprics in succession but denied the divine nature both of his office and of the Church itself, were only the more spectacular examples of the heretical spirit which seemed to mark the progress of the early Enlightenment in England.

The high-church reaction to these trends reached its peak under Queen Anne when the presence on the throne of a pious and theologically conservative queen provided an additional impulse. But its force derived much from other developments, many of them connected with party politics. The Tories, who frequently described themselves as 'The Church party', depended heavily for their appeal on the sense of crisis in the Church. They also drew extensively on the emotional support of the backwoods Anglican squirearchy. For the latter, the world opened up by the Revolution brought nothing but ill. The wars of the period necessitated the heaviest direct taxation since the 1650s. A land tax of four shillings in the pound came as a heavy burden on estates already afflicted by agricultural depression. Moreover, the war for which such sacrifices were required seemed designed to benefit precisely the enemies of the gentry—the merchants, manufacturers, and above all 'monied men' most active in the commercial and financial expansion of late Stuart England. Such men, it seemed, were often religious Dissenters, escaped all but indirect taxes, and invariably pursued Whig politics. The link between the old and new party systems was sometimes tenuous. The new Tories of Anne's reign were often drawn from families with a Puritan or Whiggish background; their leader, Robert Harley, was himself one such. On the other side, the Whig Junto, whose ruthless pursuit of place and power earned them an unenviable reputation for placing party before principle, seemed unlikely descendants of the Country Whigs of 1679. But there was no doubt about the intensity of party feeling in the early eighteenth century. It perhaps reached its height in 1710 when the Whigs impeached the Tory divine, Dr Sacheverell, for preaching the old doctrine of non-resistance. The popular convulsions which followed clearly revealed the potential for political instability which the Revolution had incidentally created. The Triennial Act of 1694 had principally been designed to compel the Crown to summon Parliament regularly, in which respect it proved unnecessary. But it also provided for frequent elections, and the consequence was a period of the most intense and unremitting electoral conflict, involving ten general elections in twenty years and exceeding anything which had gone before. Moreover, the effective abolition of state censorship, with the lapsing of the Licensing Act in 1695, ensured a large and growing forum for public debate. It is no coincidence that these years witnessed the decisive stage in the establishment of Grub Street, in the emergence of the periodical press, and in the growth of a genuinely popular political audience. In general, the reign of Anne has been seen by historians as the natural backdrop to the achievement of political stability. But on the evidence available to contemporaries it seemed rather to suggest that the price of limited monarchy and financial security was political chaos.

The Rise of Robinocracy

The Hanoverian Accession in 1714 brought new tensions to an already strained situation. While Anne lived, it had been possible, in terms of sentiment if not of logic, to consider her as a true Stuart occupying the throne in some sense in trust for her family. With the arrival of a German-speaking Elector of Hanover, strongly committed to intervention abroad and Whiggism at home, such pretences became difficult to sustain. From a dynastic standpoint everything was to play for in 1714. Many urged the Pretender to consider that London was worth the abandonment of the mass; had James III returned to the Anglican fold he would plainly have strengthened the chances of a second Stuart Restoration. Without this personal sacrifice, the Jacobite Rebellion of 1715 proved a damp squib. France, after the death of Louis XIV in the same year, was in no position to involve herself in English adventures. Even in Scotland, where the rebellion had its seat and indeed its heart, the prospects for the Stuarts were not particularly promising. 'The Scottish Union, concluded in 1708 in an atmosphere of considerable urgency, had taken much of the sting out of the succession problem. Many Scots mourned the loss of their national Parliament and thereby their independence. But the Union was shrewdly designed to preserve Scottish legal and ecclesiastical institutions, while simultaneously offering real commercial benefits through incorporation in England's imperial system. In these circumstances, the failure of the '15 was to all intents and purposes a foregone conclusion.

If the Old Pretender missed his chance, so in a different sense did his apparently successful rival, George I. By the latter part of Anne's reign, the unpopularity of the war, the electoral appeal of the 'Church in Danger', and not least the queen's own irritation with the Junto Whigs, had placed the Tories firmly in the saddle. For most of them the interests of the established Church took precedence over sentimental attachment to the Stuart dynasty. A judiciously bipartisan policy on the part of the new regime, on the lines of William III's tactics in 1689, would have done much to ease the transition of 1714. Instead, George I displayed all too clearly his readiness to make the Hanoverian succession the exclusive property of the Whigs. The years 1714–21 witnessed a campaign for Whiggish dominance which comprehensively alienated the Tories, made the dangers of the Jacobite Rebellion greater than they need have been, and generally threatened to reshape the Revolution settlement. First the Septennial Act was passed, ensuring that the new Whig government would not have to face an unmanageable electorate until the greater part of its work was complete. It was rumoured that, when that time came, the Whigs would remove all statutory restraints on the duration of Parliaments, making possible the revival of 'long' or 'pensioner' Parliaments. At the same time, the means by which the Tories of Anne's reign had endeavoured to shackle Dissent, the Occasional Conformity and Schism Acts, were first suspended and then in 1718 repealed altogether. A Universities Bill was designed to give the Crown complete control of Fellowships and Scholarships in Oxford and Cambridge, with a view to transforming the principal nurseries of the Church and the professions into Whig preserves. Above all the Peerage Bill of 1719 was projected to restrict the House of Lords to approximately its existing size. This would have ensured permanent Whig hegemony in the Upper House, regardless of any change of mind on the part of the monarch, and provided the Whigs with a built-in check on legislation affecting their interests. With this programme, there went a steady, systematic purge of Tories in the lord-lieutenancies and commissions of the peace, in the armed forces, and in the civil service at all levels.

Complete success in this great enterprise would have created a system much like that which emerged in Sweden at this time, and which condemned that country to fifty years of national impotence and aristocratic factionalism. It would have established an oligarchy as unlimited as that absolute monarchy which generations of seventeenth-century Englishmen had so dreaded. It would also have made virtually impossible one of the eighteenth century's most characteristic achievements, a stable yet flexible political structure. That it failed owed much to the divisions among the Whigs themselves. Their plans proceeded relatively smoothly while the great Whig families united to crush their opponents during the early years of George I's reign. But this union proved short-lived. The new king's foreign policy caused severe strains by its blatant use of England's naval power to secure Hanover's Baltic ambitions. There was also an increasingly bitter struggle for pre-eminence within the ministry. The eventual result, in 1717, was the Whig split, which placed Walpole and Townshend in opposition and left Stanhope and Sunderland more firmly ensconced at court than ever. Palace politics were also subject to upheaval. The king's son, the future George II, and his wife Princess Caroline, clearly indicated their intention of siding with Townshend and thereby began a long tradition of political intrigue by Hanoverian heirs to the throne. In this situation there was little hope of completing the grandiose plans of Stanhope for the promised land of Whiggism. In the House of Commons Walpole himself played a leading part in defeating the Peerage Bill and forcing the abandonment of the Universities Bill. Any hope the ministry had of saving something from the wreckage of their plans was lost soon after in the South Sea Bubble.

In retrospect, there is a certain inevitability about the South Sea Bubble and the general financial crash which went with it. It seems to bring to a fitting conclusion the intense and inflated commercialism which had accompanied the rise of the 'monied interest' in the preceding years. Yet initially there was much to be said for the scheme which caused this convulsion. The financial interests represented in the Bank of England had enjoyed a more than favourable return on their investments during the wars, and there was obviously room for greater competition between the nation's creditors. The Tory ministers of Queen Anne's reign had indeed encouraged the formation of the South Sea Company in 1711 with a view to providing an effective alternative to the Whig Bank. Moreover, there was little doubt that the funds existed, not merely in the City, but among smaller savers generally, for a more extended and more equitable investment in the public debt. The South Sea Company's scheme of 1719 seemed well calculated to redistribute the National Debt while offering better terms to the national

Exchequer. The difficulties began not with the essential logic of the scheme but with the many and varied interests involved in it. For the Directors of the Company, and especially the inner group which initiated the project, there was the need to make a substantial profit not merely for themselves but for the many courtiers, ministers, and MPs whose support was politically essential to secure acceptance of their proposals. That support was bought at a high price in terms of stock supplied on favourable terms, or even stock granted by way of open bribery. In short, many of those involved in the management of the South Sea Scheme had a strong interest in quick profits, which could only be achieved by boosting the Company's potential far beyond competing investment possibilities. Such an exercise depended heavily on the attractions of the Company's trade in the south seas. The Anglo-Spanish treaty of 1713 had given the Company a monopoly of the Spanish slave-trade and a valuable share in the Spanish American market for European goods. In theory, this offered the most promising prospects. In practice, the difficulties of managing this far-flung trade from London were to prove immense, and they were not rendered less by the often bitter conflicts between the British and Spanish governments. The trade could not have proved profitable in the short run, and even with time it could hardly fulfil the wild expectations raised in 1719. But realities were quickly forgotten in the mania for speculation which prevailed in the early months of 1720. Provided the stock was rising, new speculators were constantly encouraged to invest, permitting those who had already purchased to unload their holdings at a handsome profit. The constant inflow of funds justified new issues of stock and increasingly vociferous assertions of the durability of the investment, not to say still more generous pay-offs to the politicians. In this situation, created by a corrupt regime, a naïve investing public, and a well-established National Debt, the inevitable happened. The bubble grew steadily, encouraging still more fraudulent bubbles in ever more implausible projects as it grew. When confidence eventually failed and the bubble burst the consequences were catastrophic, particularly for those who had sold substantial assets in land or other forms of property to buy at absurdly inflated prices. Little could be done for these sufferers, by no means drawn only from the wealthiest classes. Parliament rushed through a statute severely restricting joint-stock companies for the future, but this was shutting the stable door after the horse had bolted. More dramatic action was needed to minimize the damage to the regime. The king and the Prince of Wales were publicly reconciled. The opposition Whigs were welcomed back into office, Townshend to set about cultivating the goodwill of the king's mistress the duchess of Kendal, Walpole to push through the Commons a solution for the Bubble crisis which would at least protect the National Debt and save the face of the court In this task, which earned him an enduring reputation for 'screening' corruption and fraud in high places, Walpole was in one sense aided by the very gravity of the situation. Many of those implicated in the murky transactions of 1720 were Tories who had no more enthusiasm than their Whig counterparts for public exposure. Moreover the Bubble was part of an international crisis with matching disasters in Paris and Amsterdam; it was not implausible to lay some of the blame on impersonal financial forces unconnected with individuals in the City or at court. In any event the king's ministers were, with the exception of two or three suitable scapegoats, permitted to get away with their crimes. For Walpole all this represented a great political triumph, fittingly capped by the fortuitous elimination of his rivals. Within two years, both Stanhope and Sunderland had died, leaving the way open for a new era of Walpolian supremacy, or as his opponents were to term it 'Robinocracy'.

Contemporaries, of course, could not be expected to foresee the relative stability which lay ahead. The 1720s were troubled years, not least in the most basic terms of human health and survival. The decade began, not merely with the Bubble, but with fears of a visitation from the plague which was currently devastating the south of France and which could readily be transmitted to London by way of Marseilles and the shipping lanes. In the event, the panic proved unjustified; the strains of the disease which had periodically ravished so much of Europe since the first onset of the Black Death nearly four hundred years earlier were approaching dormancy if not extinction. But this was not obvious at the time and in any case there were less exotic, home-grown maladies which continued to exert a tenacious hold on the vital statistics of demography. The later 1720s were particularly harrowing in this respect. The first three years of George II's reign, which began in 1727, were afflicted by successive waves of smallpox and influenza-like infections, imprecisely and variously described by contemporaries as agues and fevers. The demographic consequences were clearly serious. Much of the slow and slender gain in population which had occurred since the 1670s seems to have been wiped out in what was evidently the worst mortality crisis since the 1580s. By 1731 the total population stood at about 5,200,000, a figure probably lower than that for Cromwell's England in the mid-1650s.

The sense of sickness which pervaded the period was more than physiological. The greed, fraudulence, and hysteria which had characterized the South Sea Bubble were denounced both in the press and from the pulpit as the ruling vices of the years which followed. Luxury and lavish living were seen as the causes, moral decay and dissolution as the consequences. There seemed to be striking evidence of this in the great scandals which disfigured public life at this time. A whole series of parliamentary investigations uncovered extensive corruption in high places. The trustees of the Derwentwater estates were found to have connived at the sale of forfeited Jacobite property to some of their own number at artificially low prices. The directors and officials of the Charitable Corporation, whose duty it was to provide employment and assistance for the poor, were convicted of jobbery, misappropriation, and even outright peculation. In both cases, prominent MPs and supporters of the government were implicated. More sensational still was the impeachment of the Lord Chancellor, Lord Macclesfield, for

organizing the sale of judicial offices. Even his ministerial colleagues declined to defend him when it emerged that this
flourishing branch of commercial law had been financed from
the proceeds of private property entrusted to the care of Chan-
cery. That the guardians of equity should thus be caught in the
act of infringing it seemed peculiarly shocking to an age which
entertained a profound respect for rights of property. Moreover, public misdeeds could readily be matched by private ones.
Crime, a distorting mirror of society, but a mirror none the
less, seemed to become ever more organized, more commercial,
and more cynical. Jonathan Wild, the master thief-taker, was a
fitting representative of his time. Most of his profits were
gained by restoring to their owners the goods stolen by his own
minions. His success depended heavily on the corrupt collaboration of JPs and their officers in the metropolis. His was
only one growth sector in the flourishing economy of crime.
Poachers in the royal forests were often well-organized, systematic suppliers to the London market. The smugglers of the
south and east coasts pursued market principles and economies
of scale, again with the frequent co-operation of officials and
the public at large. The authorities made somewhat desperate
attempts to combat these threats. Wild was brought to justice
on a technicality. His execution in 1725 was to ensure his place
in popular mythology. The poachers of Windsor Forest and
elsewhere were the subject of new legislation, the draconian
Black Act of 1723. They have had to wait until the twentieth
century to achieve the status of folk-heroes, in their case
bestowed by historians intent on treating them as authentic
representatives of a popular culture. The smugglers seemed to
flourish almost in proportion to the government's efforts to
suppress them; at their most active in the 1730s they were
capable of mounting pitched battles with George II's dragoons
in their heroic service to a consumer society.

   For this was what was emerging in early Hanoverian England. In this respect the South Sea Bubble is best seen not as the
grand finale of post-Revolution England, but rather as a spec-

tacular curtain-raiser to the prosperity, vulgarity, and commercialism of the mid-eighteenth century. The theatrical metaphor is peculiarly appropriate, for the period has a special significance in the history of the performing arts. The 1720s and 1730s witnessed a considerable expansion in the London theatre and an increasingly political role for it. Until the court took action to obtain extensive powers of censorship in 1737 it was the forum, along with the press generally, for a mounting campaign of criticism of the kind of society which seemed to have emerged during and after the Bubble. Nothing expressed such criticism more effectively than John Gay's *Beggar's Opera*, the great success of 1728. Whether the opera was actually intended as a political satire is uncertain, but it is significant of the contemporary climate of opinion that it was instantly accepted as such. Gay's message fitted well into the prevailing concern with illusion and unreality. It clearly depicted the court of George II as a kind of thieves' kitchen; the morality of the ruling class was put on par with that of the London underworld. It was a point which Fielding was to reinforce by means of his unflattering comparison of Jonathan Wild with Sir Robert Walpole. It also had closely matching themes in Pope's *Dunciad*, Swift's *Gulliver's Travels*, and Bolingbroke's *Craftsman*, all products of a remarkable decade of polemical satire. Many of its elements were familiar ones: the retreat into classicism, the appeal to country values, the attraction of the rural idyll, above all the incessant criticism of the supposedly synthetic, moneyed world of early eighteenth-century commercialism. In these respects the literary and journalistic invective of the Walpole era can be seen, indeed, as the final, most violent surge of a tide which had been flowing for many years. But in inspiration for the future, or constructive analysis of alternative possibilities, it was manifestly deficient.

When Gay's audience glimpsed in Macheath the very essence of Walpolian politics, they seized upon one of the most significant aspects of the period—the close connection, seen if not established, between the political character of the Hanoverian regime and the supposed ills of contemporary society. With a few exceptions (notably the cartoonist William Hogarth, who reserved most of his energies for satirizing manners and morals), the intellectual and artistic élite of London was remarkably unanimous in its view that Walpole was the arch-villain of the piece. His characteristic image was that of a *parvenu* Norfolk placeman, enriched by a career of systematic corruption (he had been prosecuted by the Tories for official peculation in 1712) and elevated to supreme power for his utter lack of principle and total submission to the views of the court. Before 1727, his brother-in-law, Lord Townshend, had shared both his power and his unpopularity. But the death of George I and the accession of a new king placed him clearly in the full glare of public attention. By his adroit management of George II and more especially Queen Caroline, Walpole elbowed out all rivals for power, including, in 1730, Townshend himself. As a result he soon achieved a lonely eminence such as none had enjoyed, perhaps, since Danby in the 1670s. His hegemony inevitably drew the full fire of Grub Street on his personal position. He was the Great Man, the English Colossus, the Man Mountain. He also appeared as the perfect representative of the politics of illusion—the Norfolk trickster, the Savoy Rareeshowman, Palinurus the magician, Merlin the wizard, the Screenmaster-General and so on. Both his mastery of the irascible and unpredictable George II and his control of a previously unmanageable Parliament were protrayed in countless broadsides and prints as the arts of a veritable political conjuror.

At the time and ever since, the true basis of Walpole's success has been traced to his skilful use of influence and even bribery. The stability which seems to mark the period and to separate it from the political chaos of earlier years can be viewed, on this reading, as the natural culmination of forces working in favour of the executive. The expansion of government as a result of the wars, especially the vast machinery created to operate the new financial system, plainly generated a considerable quantity of new patronage. Moreover, the overwhelming necessity for post-revolution governments to obtain a working majority in the Commons provided a strong incentive to use this patronage for the purposes of parliamentary management. Hence the emergence of a much larger, much more disciplined Court and Treasury party, capable of bridging the ancient gap between Crown and Commons and inaugurating a new era of harmony between executive and legislature. It is an attractive theory, but not all the premisses are secure and not all the conclusions inescapable. Walpole's principles of management were far from novel. At least since the reign of Charles II, they had been employed by successive ministers to maintain a substantial court party in the House of Commons. Placemanship and careerism, not to say widespread evidence of corruption, had marked the reign of Anne as much as that of her successors. In some respects, indeed, the peaceful years of Walpole's ministry reduced the amount of patronage available. It is true enough that both Walpole himself and his effective successor Henry Pelham were adroit managers, and that both welded the court party into an exceptionally efficient instrument of control. But it needed more than patronage to create the classical parliamentary system of Georgian England.

This is not to deny Walpole's own inimitable talents. As a courtier he was without compare. His manipulation of the queen and (partly through her) of the king was a consummate mixture of flattery, cajolery, and bullying, brilliantly described in the memoirs of Lord Hervey, whose intimacy with Queen Caroline gave him ample opportunity to witness it. But winning courtiers were nothing new. What was more striking was the unusual combination of gifts which permitted him to handle MPs with equal skill. His decision to remain in the House of Commons as first minister was quite critical in this respect. Where previous ministers had traditionally departed to the Lords Walpole made a point of remaining in the chamber which ultimately controlled the purse-strings of government. As a debater he was somewhat crude (not necessarily a disadvantage), skilled, and extremely effective. As a conciliator, his capacity for ascertaining and implementing the views of the typical country gentleman was outstanding. But most important of all were his policies, which differed profoundly from the partisan programme of his old Whig colleagues. His desire to avoid exacerbating ancient animosities was particularly marked in his treatment of the Church. With the assistance of Indemnity Acts the Dissenters were left to enjoy their freedom of worship and even some measure of local power. But there was no serious attempt to break the Anglican monopoly in principle, and the repeal of the Test and Corporation Acts had to wait another hundred years. Nor was there any serious talk of wholesale changes elsewhere, in the corporations, the universities, or indeed in Parliament itself. The new Whig policy of peace with France became under Walpole a policy of peace with everyone, carrying with it the priceless advantage of low taxation. In theory the Whig supremacy continued unabated. In practice Walpole subtly transformed the basis of the Hanoverian regime. The politics of coercion gave way to those of consensus; the objective of an exclusive oligarchy was replaced by the uninspiring but solid appeal of a ruling coalition open to anyone prepared to pay lip-service to undefined 'Revolution principles'.

Even without Walpole the Hanoverian regime would eventually have had an important impact on the pattern of politics. For simply in terms of corruption it was not the novelty of Walpole's management which counted, but rather the extent to which patronage was channelled in one direction. Before 1714, uncertain or inconsistent policies on the part of the court had made the calculations of placemen and patrons exceedingly difficult. From the boroughmonger at the apex of the electoral pyramid to the humble exciseman or common councillor at its base, it was far from clear where the means to profit and power lay. Much of the instability of party politics under Queen Anne arose from the resulting oscillations. After 1715 this problem was resolved for more than a generation by one simple and central fact of public life. Both George I and George II objected to the inclusion of Tories in their ministries, and with the exception of the short-lived Broad Bottom Administration in 1743, a product of the instability which followed Walpole's fall, the Tory party remained in the wilderness for more than forty years. Paradoxically, this proscription made ministerial stability more secure. Court Tories were more determinedly courtiers than they were Tories, and the prospect of permanent exclusion from place and profit was more than many could bear. Moreover, Walpole's form of Whiggism was exceptionally un-demanding and there were many whose families had previously sided with the Tories who found little difficulty in subscribing to the new Whig principles. This particularly was the case with those who from interest or instinct gravitated naturally towards the politics of courts. By the 1730s the close boroughs of Corn-wall, divided between Whigs and Tories at the beginning of the century, were dependable Whig preserves. In the Lords only a handful of Tory peers continued loyal to their friends in the Commons, though in 1712 Harley had achieved a Tory major-ity there. The change was not sudden or spectacular but it was steady and sustained, and some of the most important political names of the eighteenth century were part of it, including both the Pitt and the Fox families.

The stability of the political scene under Walpole and Pelham was unquestionably a major achievement of the Hanoverian system; but it is important not to exaggerate its extent. Politics in George II's reign did not descend into the torpor with which they are often associated. For the price of Hanoverian iden-tification with Whiggism, albeit a somewhat watery Whiggism, was the permanent alienation of the die-hard 'country' Tory families. These families, though they rarely produced politicians of the first rank, maintained a certain resilience in opposition and provided an important focus for other potentially hostile elements. They made life difficult and unpleasant for those of their comrades who did defect; for example, when one of their aristocratic leaders, Earl Gower, joined Henry Pelham, the re-sult at the general election of 1747 was rioting of almost unparalleled ferocity in Gower's home county of Staffordshire. In the counties, indeed, the Tories had their heartland. Among the forty-shilling freeholders of the county electorates, particularly in the Midlands, the west country, and Wales, they received consistent and even increasing support. Elsewhere they were influential if not dominating. The Toryism of the Church was bound to be diluted by the persistent drip of Whig jobbery, but one of the great seminaries of the Church, the university of Oxford, remained loyal to the Anglican gentry, and there was sufficient ecclesiastical patronage in the hands of the Tory families to maintain a powerful interest. In substantial cities there were also promising reservoirs of potential opposition to the regime. In London, Bristol, Norwich, and Newcastle, for instance, there was a long tradition of popular participation in politics, and much combustible material for Tory incendiaries. The Walpole system was too widely based to be considered a narrow oligarchy, but while a significant portion of the landed and clerical classes and a large body of middle- and lower-class opinion in the towns opposed it, the stability of the age could be more apparent than real.

Naturally enough, the conditions for genuine crisis were created only when the regime itself was divided. By the early 1730s Walpole was faced by a dangerous alliance of rivals at court. Their opportunity came with his celebrated attempt to extend the excise system, a project which was financially sound but which awakened the deepest and most violent antipathy among those numerous Englishmen who detested new taxes and feared the expansion of the government's bureaucracy. Only Walpole's readiness to withdraw his scheme in 1733 and the solid support of George II against his court rivals saved his administration; even so, the general election of 1734 produced a widespread reaction against him and a severely reduced majority in the House of Commons. An even more serious situation arose four years later. The powerful out-of-doors agitation which demanded an aggressive stance towards the Spanish Empire in 1738 and 1739 was all the more dangerous because it had support from Frederick Prince of Wales. The consequent alliance of alienated Tories, discontented Whigs, hostile business men, popular politicians, and the heir to the throne was dangerous indeed and eventually it was not only to force Walpole into a war which he profoundly disliked, but even to bring him down. The problem of the reversionary interest was particularly alarming; it was, until Frederick's death in 1751, to pose Pelham the same problems which it posed Walpole.

Even without these internal strains, the Whig supremacy faced considerable opposition. The Jacobite threat was probably exaggerated; it may be doubted whether many of those who toasted 'the king over the water' would actually have risked either their property or their lives for the House of Stuart. None the less, the more committed among them had some encouragement. The War of Austrian Succession (1740–8) found Britain involved, not merely against Spain overseas, but against a powerful Bourbon coalition on the Continent. In that war George II seemed primarily concerned to protect his beloved electorate; the consequent clash with domestic interests, and above all the unpopularity of investing British money and British blood in Germany and the Netherlands, gave patriot politicians ample ammunition for attacks on the regime. Walpole had predicted long before that warfare would mean a struggle for the English succession on English soil, and so it proved. When the Jacobite invasion came in 1745, it revealed the full extent of the danger to the Hanoverian dynasty. By European standards, the British standing army was tiny; even the small and ill-assorted force which the Young Pretender brought right into the heart of the English Midlands in December 1745 plainly stretched the defenders to the limit. An effective militia, without Tory support, had long since been abandoned; many of the country gentry offered at best sullen neutrality. The ferocious terror which was deployed against the Scottish Highlanders after the Jacobite army had been pushed back and finally crushed at Culloden was a measure of the alarm and even panic which had gripped the authorities in

London. In these respects, as in others, the crisis of 1745 provides a useful corrective to excessively bland portrayals of the essential complacency of the Whig system. The customary picture of political apathy and aristocratic elegance can be a misleading one. It hardly fits the ragged but bloody progress of the rebels in 1745, nor do the relatively sedate years of the early 1750s altogether bear it out.

Pelham, for example, whose adroit management had steered his country safely if somewhat ignominiously out of the war and whose financial acumen did much to put the National Debt on a more secure basis thereafter, proved capable of misjudging the political climate. His Jew Bill of 1753, designed to soften the civil disabilities of the Jewish community in Britain, provoked a torrent of high-church hostility and intolerance and compelled him to repeal the offending measure before he could be punished for it in the general election of 1754. Again, the Jacobite alarms and excursions were far from over. As late as 1753 London was regaled with the spectacle of a Jacobite rebel being publicly hanged; in some respects, no doubt, politics in the eighteenth century was more polite, but it was not invariably so.

Industry and Idleness

The death throes of Jacobitism coincided chronologically with the passing away of pre-industrial society, for conventional accounts of the immense economic growth and change described as the Industrial Revolution locate its birth firmly in the mid-eighteenth century. Yet the period which in retrospect seems to have provided the platform for industrial take-off was widely regarded at the time as one of worrying recession, and continues to present problems of evaluation. In the 1730s and 1740s agricultural prices were exceptionally low; some important manufacturing regions, particularly the old textile centres, suffered serious unemployment and unrest. But there were also more promising developments. Low food prices permitted higher spending on consumer goods and thereby encouraged the newer industries, particularly in the Midlands. If agriculture was frequently depressed by these prices it was also stimulated by them, in East Anglia for example, to increase production. The improved techniques of mixed farming often associated with the age of 'Turnip' Townshend do not belong exclusively to this period, but their importance was certainly more widely appreciated. In other sectors there was very marked advance. For instance, the 1730s witnessed one of the most striking developments in the history of transport—the construction of a nation-wide turnpike system. Before 1730, only a handful of turnpike trusts had been established. Most main roads, including the Great North Road beyond Northamptonshire and almost the whole of the Great West Road, depended for their maintenance on those unfortunate parishes which happened to lie in the immediate vicinity. The roads of early Georgian England, subjected to the immense strain of rapidly-growing passenger traffic and ever more burdensome freight services between major centres of consumption, were rightly considered a national disgrace. Turnpike trusts were a neat, if not always popular, solution, which permitted the injection of substantial sums of locally raised capital into repair and maintenance, on the security of a carefully graduated system of tolls. The heyday of the trusts lay in the four middle decades of the century. They testified strongly to the vitality of the provinces, with a large proportion of the new roads in the north and in the West Midlands; by 1770, when the canals were beginning to offer stiff competition for freight, they offered a genuinely national network of relatively efficient transport. The effect on journey times was dramatic. Major provincial centres such as York, Manchester, and Exeter were well over three days' travel from London in the 1720s; by 1780 they could be reached in not much more than twenty-four hours. Significantly these reductions, which applied to almost all important routes, seem to have stretched contemporary transport technology to the limit; they were subject to little further improvement until about

1820, when Macadam and Telford were to achieve further striking savings.

The development of the turnpikes would not have been possible without a great expansion of inland consumption, trade, and capital. But the internal growth implied in these years was more than matched by expansion overseas. Again contemporary appearances could be misleading. Patriot politicians continued to hold before the public an essentially old-fashioned view of empire. Colonies still tended to be seen primarily as valuable sources of raw materials, as dumping grounds for surplus population, or as means of adding to the nation's stock of bullion. The jewels in the imperial crown were the West Indies, with their sugar plantations; the Anglo-Spanish War of 1739, like its predecessors, was seen as a means of breaking into the eldorado of South America, with enticing prospects of gold, silver, and tropical products. Yet in retrospect it is clear that Britain's overseas trade was being recast in the direction of a quite new kind of empire. The dynamic export markets lay increasingly outside Europe, notably in North America. Textiles, the traditional staple, benefited by this redirection, but the growth was still more marked in the newer manufacturing sectors associated particularly with the metal industries, in the production of household commodities, tools, weapons, and all kinds of utensils—in short in the vastly expanding demand for 'Birmingham goods'.

Mercantilist theories were capable of adaptation to accommodate the new trends but it took a time for the process to register clearly with contemporaries. By the 1750s, the full importance of the thirteen American colonies was beginning to be appreciated, and the eyes of businessmen and administrators alike were beginning to turn towards competition with France for dominance of the North Atlantic world. The changing emphasis also had important implications in domestic terms. The growth of Georgian London was rapid, and its place as the greatest and most dynamic city in the Western world was already secure. But the fact was that in strictly comparative terms London was less important. A large share of the new trade in the Americas went to new or growing ports in the west, notably Liverpool, Bristol, Glasgow, and for a short but spectacular burst of commercial activity, Whitehaven. The industrial hinterland of these ports, the Severn Valley and West Midlands, the Yorkshire and Lancashire regions, and the west of Scotland, were decisively shifting the industrial base of the country away from the south, east, and west, towards the north and Midlands.

This shift is clearly seen in the demographic trends of the period. After the disasters of the 1720s, population had started growing again, albeit on a very gently rising plateau in the 1730s. The abortive Census proposed in 1750, had it been conducted, would probably have identified a total of about 5.8 million, half a million more than twenty years previously. By 1770 it stood at about 6.4 million, and by 1790 it was approaching 8 million. By nineteenth-century standards this was not a very impressive rate of growth. None the less it represented the crucial turning-point in modern demographic history. Much the same could be said of industrial and urban growth generally. There was no shortage of important innovations and new enterprises in the late seventeenth and early eighteenth century. But between the age of Abraham Darby and the age of Josiah Wedgwood there lay a world of difference. In this respect, the mid-century was again a watershed. The familiar giants of the early industrial revolution, Boulton and Watt, Garbett, Arkwright, Wedgwood himself, made their mark on the national consciousness in the 1760s and 1770s, and it was at the time of the Seven Years War, in the early 1760s, that the full excitement of what was occurring for instance at Birmingham and Manchester began to register. Urban improvement itself reflected the economic growth and the widespread interest in it. Contemporaries who could remember the reign of Queen Anne and who were to live on into the last quarter of the eighteenth century cited the 1760s and 1770s as a time of extraordinary change and improvement in the material life of the cities, and

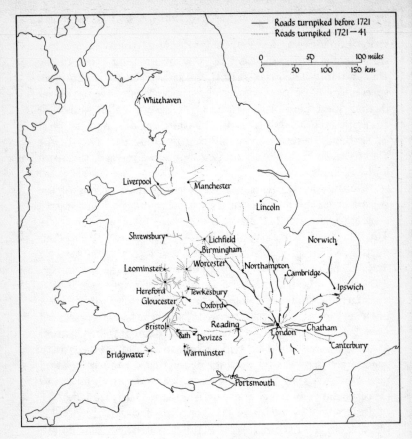

Legend:
— Roads turnpiked before 1721
······· Roads turnpiked 1721–41

THE TURNPIKE ROAD NETWORK IN 1741

also to some extent of the smaller towns. The emphasis was always on space, hygiene, and order. The expanding towns of Manchester and Glasgow were much admired by visitors for their spacious squares, and neat rows of houses and warehouses. By comparison, the cluttered townscape of the older centres, with its narrow streets and timber and thatch housing, seemed outdated and even barbarous. No town with civic self-respect neglected the chance to obtain parliamentary authority for an improvement commission, equipped with extensive powers

THE TURNPIKE ROAD NETWORK IN 1770

of rebuilding. Many of the better-preserved Georgian towns of today owe their character to this period of urban redevelopment. Perhaps the most spectacular example of imaginative town-planning occurred north of the border; Edinburgh's New Town continues to testify to the vigour of the City fathers in this respect. The capital of South Britain was not far behind. In a symbolic as well as practical act of modernization, the City of London's medieval gates were demolished in 1761. One of them, Ludgate, had been confidently restored and embellished, with further centuries of service in mind, less than thirty years previously. In nearby Westminster the biggest single project of urban redevelopment was begun at almost the same time in 1762. The Westminster Paving Commissioners and their collaborators in individual parishes were to transform the face of a vast area of the metropolis. Sewers and water-mains were extensively laid or redesigned. Streets and pedestrian walks were cobbled and paved, many for the first time. Squares were cleared, restored, and adorned with a variety of statuary and flora. Houses were systematically numbered; the old signs, colourful, but cumbersome and even dangerous to passers-by, were cleared away. By the 1780s the physical appearance of the capital, with the exception of its slums, was a source of pride to its inhabitants, and of wonder to its visitors, particularly foreigners.

Change was not restricted to cities and towns. Village architecture changed more gradually in most cases, but on the land itself new patterns were emerging. The most celebrated symptoms of the agricultural revolution, the parliamentary enclosure acts, were heavily concentrated in the second half of the eighteenth century. Their economic impact can be exaggerated, for they were statistically less significant than the relatively silent non-parliamentary enclosure which had been proceeding for decades and even centuries; moreover they were principally a feature of the regional belt running south and west from Yorkshire to Gloucestershire. But as pointers to the profitability of agriculture on marginal or convertible land, they are powerful evidence, and in their impact on the landscape they deeply impressed contemporaries. By the time of Adam Smith's *Wealth of Nations*, published in 1776, they suggested a confidence amounting almost to complacency about the continuance of economic growth. Curiously Smith himself did not altogether share this confidence. But Smith was an academic, his work was essentially one of theory rather than practical observation, and much of it had ben conceived before the more spectacular developments of the 1760s and 1770s. His countryman John

Campbell, whose *Political Survey* (1774) was an unshamed panegyric of Britain's economic progress, is in this respect a surer guide.

The gathering pace of material growth had an inevitable impact on the character of English society. To some extent the results were in line with the trends suggested by commercial diversification and the general advance of capitalism in preceding periods. In terms of social structure, therefore, the principal effect was, so to speak, to stretch the social hierarchy. Because wealth was distributed so unevenly, and because the levels and nature of taxation did so little to redistribute that wealth, real living standards rose much more dramatically in the middle and at the top of the social scale than at the bottom. In principle, this was by no means new. For example, the development of agriculture in the course of the sixteenth and seventeenth centuries had already noticeably altered the structure of the typical rural community. Enclosure, engrossing, improvement in general were gradually turning village society, characterized by the small property-owner, the freeholder or yeoman beloved of enthusiasts for Old England, into something quite new. Substantial capitalist farmers, frequently tenants of gentry landlords rather than landowners themselves, were coming to dominate an agrarian world in which all below them were increasingly reduced to landless labourers. The process has sometimes been exaggerated, for its actual incidence depended heavily on local conditions. But it certainly speeded up during the eighteenth century, and, most importantly, had a close counterpart in the development of industrial and urban society.

In this sense at least eighteenth-century England was growing into a more polarized society. Worse, the damaging consequences of polarization were far more apparent. Increased mobility, not to say the large contemporary improvement in literacy and communications generally, made worrying comparisons of rich and poor ever more obvious. The extravagant life-style of a ruling élite which seemed to live in a blaze of conspicuous consumption, and also the more modest but cumulatively more influential rise in middle-class standards of living, made the inequalities of a highly commercial, cash-based economy glaringly plain. The *malaise*, if it was a *malaise*, was at its most conspicuous in the capital. Conditions in London, with its relative shortage of well-established social restraints and conventions, its constant tendency to throw the wretchedly poor into close, but profitless, contact with the comfortably bourgeois and even the immensely rich, inevitably gave rise to moral outrage and social criticism of the kind which lives on in Fielding and Hogarth.

How much of the concern reflected an actual worsening of living conditions, it is difficult to judge. Before 1750, very low food prices, combined with the wage stability of a relatively static population, probably increased the real earnings of the poor. The fearful problems arising from the Londoner's thirst for gin—and the less damaging but at the time equally criticized liking of the poorer sort for tea—suggest that at least there was no shortage of disposable income at this time. After the mid-century, however, conditions seem to have deteriorated for many. A return to the older cycle of indifferent and even deficient harvests, together with the episodic slumps and unemployment characteristic of industrial economies, made life at the bottom of the heap a hazardous and harrowing business. Moreover, rapid population growth together with mechanical innovation helped to keep wages relatively low, and ensured that the advantages of industrial expansion were not necessarily shared with the humbler members of an emerging proletariat.

The eighteenth century was more sensitive to social problems than it has sometimes seemed, though it had no easy or comprehensive answers. The poor themselves fought back, mainly with traditional weapons in defence of an embattled economic order. Against dearth and high prices, they appealed to ancient laws restricting middlemen and monopolies. Against wage-cutting and the introduction of machinery, they organized combinations to defeat their masters, and clubs to provide an element of social insurance. In extremity, they rebelled and rioted with regularity and enthusiasm. This was a losing battle, although they were not without their victories. The landed gentry had some sympathy with popular resentment of the activities of moneyed and mercantile entrepreneurs. But the growth of a specialized market for the products of an improving agriculture was as essential to the landlord as to the provisions merchant. Similarly with the antiquated machinery of industrial relations: attempts to enforce the old apprenticeship laws were ineffective against the joint efforts of capitalist manufacturers and unskilled labourers to cheat them. A corporation which succeeded in operating such restrictive practices merely ensured that it did not share in new investment and industry. Associations received even shorter shrift. The friendly clubs, intended purely to provide pensions and sickness benefits, were encouraged by the upper orders. But combinations (or trade unions), even when directed against the more manifest injustices of eighteenth-century employers, such as the use of truck in the west-country clothing industry, were frequently repressed. Where they sometimes succeeded, as in the London tailoring trade, or in the royal dockyards, it was a tribute to the determination of well-established industrial groups. In most of the new industries the manufacturer swept all before him.

The most extreme manifestation of lower-class discontent was in some respects the most tolerated, no doubt because it was seen by paternalistic rulers as a necessary if regrettable safety valve. The measures used to suppress riots were rarely excessive, and punishment was used in an exemplary way on a small number of those involved. Even then, it was often surprisingly light if the provocation seemed extreme and there were no serious implications. Election riots, indeed, were regarded for most of the period as largely unavoidable; in a tumultuous town such as Coventry, with a large electorate and active involvement by those who were not even electors, they were a predictable feature of every election. The recurrent food riots associated with periods of dearth like the mid-1750s and the mid-1760s were also treated as a more or less necessary, if unwelcome, aspect of country life. Within certain limits, there was a wide tolerance in such matters. For instance, the fury of the Spitalfields silk weavers in London in 1765 (when it was believed that the duke of Bedford had worsened their plight by his support for the importation of French silks) brought about something like a full-scale siege of Bedford House. The riots were serious enough to warrant the use of troops, yet even polite London society saw nothing incongruous in treating them as an interesting diversion, worthy of personal inspection from the sidelines. Persistence, of course, was liable to lead to sterner consequences. Thus, the initial riots against turnpikes in the 1730s were treated with relative good humour, and even a hint of encouragement from some among the propertied classes who resented tolls as much as their lowlier compatriots. But exemplary sentences inevitably followed. Moreover, from the 1760s there were hints of a changing attitude towards popular disturbances. John Wilkes's protracted and controversial campaign in defence of electoral rights and the freedom of the press produced violent demonstrations on the streets. The consequent clashes with authority in the name of 'Wilkes and Liberty' had too many political implications to be viewed with complacency. The anti-papist Gordon riots of 1780, which for the first time produced a real state of terror in London, marked a further important stage in this process. It needed only the French Revolution in the following decade to complete the destruction of the old tolerance and to install the popular riot among the bugbears of the propertied mind.

There were no permanent solutions to the problems engendered by the quantitative growth and qualitative impoverishment of the lowest sort. Poor relief in the eighteenth century continued to be operated on the basis of the Elizabethan Poor Law and the 1662 Act of Settlements. At their worst, these would have put the life of a poor labourer and his family on a par with or perhaps below that of an American slave or a Russian serf. Poor relief might involve the barest minimum of subsistence dependent on ungenerous neighbours, or sojourn in a poor house with consequent exposure to a ruthless master who drew his income from the systematic exploitation of those in his charge. The laws of settlement provided for compulsory residence in the parish of birth for those not occupying a house worth at least £10 per annum, a not insubstantial sum. In practice, these draconian regulations were less forbidding. Poor relief was a major item in the expenditure of most parishes and by the late eighteenth century was already growing at an alarming rate. If frequently extended to regular outdoor relief and to some extent took account of the rising cost and the rising standard of living. The settlement laws were enforced only to a limited extent. Unhappily their chief victims were women, children, and the old, precisely those who were likely to be a burden on the parish to which they fled. But, even so, restrictions on movement by the second half of the century in reality were slight. The immense labour requirements of industry could hardly have been met if there had been any serious attempt to implement them.

Propertied people felt strongly about the poor in this as in other ages. But they felt still more strongly about crime. For a commercialized society provided ever more temptations, and ever more provocation by way of encouragement to lawlessness. The flashier forms of criminality, such as highway robbery, or the most sociologically interesting, such as offences against the game laws, have traditionally attracted most attention. But the vast majority of crime was one form or another of petty theft, an offence against propertied values which seemed to present a constantly growing threat, particularly in the urban areas. Against this tide of illegality, exaggerated no doubt, but real enough for all that, property in this period had few defences. Urban crime cried out for effective police forces offering a high chance of detection and conviction (if it did not cry out for kinder cures!). But a police force would have presented many dangers, not least its potential use in terms of political patronage. Moreover the continuing threat represented by any organized force at the command of government was taken very seriously. Few would have seen the point in keeping a standing army to the minimum while permitting a more novel and no less sinister force to spring up in its stead. In consequence, with few and partial exceptions, for example the efforts of the Fielding brothers in London, the period witnessed no significant improvement in this area. Rather, the authorities were driven back on sheer deterrence, the threat of transportation or death even for relatively insignificant offences. This was the period of the proliferation of capital sentences for minor crimes, against which early nineteenth-century reformers were to fulminate. It was in fact the only logical means to stem the flow of crimes against property. Even so it proved self-defeating. For juries would not convict and judges would not condemn in any but the clearest cases. The statistics of conviction are small compared with the actual numbers of offences. Even when the death sentence had been pronounced there was a strong chance of a reprieve at the request of the judge, or at the behest of a highly-placed patron. In this way, the processes of justice inevitably sank into the general welter of inconsistent policy and political manipulation which marked the period.

If the poor looked to the State in vain, they looked to the Church with but faint hope. The Church of the eighteenth century has a poor reputation for what would today be called social policy. Entrenched as it was in the patronage structure of the Georgian world, it could hardly be expected to offer a systematic challenge to prevailing attitudes. But it does not altogether deserve its reputation. The sheer volume of eighteenth-century charity is sometimes forgotten. No doubt this is largely because it was overwhelmingly voluntary, and informal. Without the official or state papers which accompany the exercise of charity in a later or even an earlier age it can easily vanish from sight. Yet in terms of the endowment and maintenance of a host of institutions for education, health, and recreation the record is a striking one. It was marked by a frequently patronizing attitude, and motivated in part by an anxiety to keep at bay the social and political threat of the dispossessed. But this is not uncharacteristic of other periods, and the sheer quantity remains surprising. Subscription and association—the central features of this process—built schools, endowed hospitals, established poor houses, supervised benefit societies. In this the Church, or rather the churches, were heavily involved. Not the least active was a class reviled by later reformers, the dignitaries of the Anglican Establishment—its bishops, archdeacons, deans, and canons.

There was, however, a paradox about the Church's position in the eighteenth century. The influence of 'natural' religion in the early part of the century had produced a growing emphasis on works rather than faith. Christians were those who behaved like Christians, and charity was the most obvious expression of religious devotion. But rational religion, however benevolent, did not offer much spiritual consolation to those who lacked the education or the intellect to be rational. The spiritual energy of all the main churches manifestly wilted under the impact of latitudinarian tendencies. Mainstream Dissent, tortured by the theological tensions which arose from the deist challenge to the doctrine of the Trinity, visibly declined as a force in popular life and retreated for the moment at least to its traditional support among the urban middle class. The Church in the rural areas continued its somewhat erratic work, dependent as ever on the residence and personal commitment of a portion of its clergy. In the towns it was all too prone to withdraw, or to appeal, like Dissenters, to the polite middle-class congregations who could afford to supplement the poor town livings and to beautify or rebuild churches.

It was left to that rebellious daughter of the Church, the Methodist movement, to offer the poor recompense in the next world for their sufferings in this. The many facets and connections of Wesleyan Methodism make it difficult to generalize about its importance. John Wesley himself was an Oxford don of high-church views and unenlightened politics. Yet to many his influence seemed to express something of the Puritan spirit of seventeenth-century religion. His own spiritual journey was tempestuous and marked by the highest degree of what could easily be seen as recklessness and self-will. But the organization and discipline which he bestowed on his followers verged on despotism. In theological terms, Wesley was an Arminian; but Calvinism exercised a far-reaching effect on the Methodist movement. Indeed Wesley was preceded in the field by Calvinists such as Griffith Jones and Howell Harris in Wales, and George Whitefield in England. To their enemies, all such men seemed dangerous, even seditious characters. Field-preaching could be seen as an open attack on the parish clergy's monopoly of the pulpit; from the vantage point of lay authority, Wesley's readiness to preach his saving message to all ranks and degrees made squires and shires shake. Yet his political views were positively authoritarian, and he offered no challenge to social order. Through his attitudes and those of his followers ran only one concern: the total availability of the evangelist's salvation to all, above all to the poor, to the outcast communities of mining and manufacturing England, neglected by more fashionable divines. It is possible to exaggerate his achievement, for at his death there can hardly have been more than about seventy to eighty thousand committed Methodists. Yet the alarm and controversy to which his turbulent life and travels gave rise suggests the extent of his impact on Georgian society. Methodists were accused of an infinity of sins, some of them mutually incompatible. Their preachers were both papists and Puritans, Jacobites and republicans; they ravished wives or influenced them to give up all fleshly pleasures; they coveted other men's goods or denied them the use of worldly possessions. The sheer multiplicity of the charges against Methodism makes it obvious that Wesley touched a tender spot on the contemporary conscience and exposed an embarrassing deficiency in its pattern of beliefs.

The Making of Middle England

The impression confirmed by the early history of the Methodist movement is very much one of considerable social strains and problems. But it is possible to over-colour the general picture. For one thing it was widely believed at the time that English society avoided the worst of extremes. Foreigners were struck by the flexibility and cohesion of the English social fabric, not by its tensions and rigidities. A succession of French visitors, from Voltaire to the Abbé Grosley, testified in print to the lack of 'caste' in this country, and especially to the ease with which individuals could move up and down the social ladder. In particular the absence of aristocratic privileges and advantages compared with the Continent earned their applause. Peers might be tried by the House of Lords, but when they went to the gallows they suffered publicly like common criminals. When Lord Ferrers was executed for murdering his servant in 1760 his fate was widely construed as clear evidence that in crime and in death alike the law of England made no distinctions. In a matter of less moment but perhaps no less significance, Grosley was astonished to discover that the tolls on the new turnpikes were paid regardless of rank and without remission for noblemen. Moreover the degradation and dearth which threatened the lives of the urban poor seemed preferable by far to the conditions of French or German peasants. The English labourer (though it must be admitted that commentators usually meant the London labourer) seemed well paid, well fed and extraordinarily independent and articulate. Most important of all perhaps was the emphasis laid by foreigners on the flexible definition of the English gentleman. Anyone, it appeared, who chose to dress like a gentleman was treated like one. Middle-class, even lower-class Londoners aped the fashions, manners, and opinions of polite society. This, it seems clear, was the authentic mark of a society in which all social values, distinctions, and customs gave way before the sovereign power of cash. England was the outstanding example in eighteenth-century Europe of a plutocratic society.

The nature of this plutocracy provides a crucial clue to the social stability of the period. On the face of it there was little evidence that the basic structure of property-ownership was changing dramatically. There was no striking surge of bourgeois capital into land, no great expropriation of the landed aristocracy or gentry. The steady assimilation of small professional and business families altered the precise make-up of the landed class without significantly affecting its overall character. Higher up the scale, the eighteenth century witnessed some strengthening and consolidation of the great landowners. But land was only one form of property and not necessarily the most important. Even at the beginning of the century the primacy of land was diminishing. Estimates of national income at the time of the Glorious Revolution suggest that agriculture contributed nearly a half of the total. But the proportion was changing; by 1780 it was probably down to a third. In fact, the land itself was merely part of the general commercialization of the English economy; in its exploitation and its improvement, it was increasingly treated exactly like an investment in stock, in trade, and in manufacturing. It was noticeable that, whereas temporary agrarian depressions had little significance for trade, the converse did not hold; commercial recessions had extremely grave implications for land prices. In the American War, when overseas trade suffered a disastrous slump, the effect was instantly seen on property values, with serious political consequences. If the landed classes had owned the greater part of non-landed property, the situation would have been very different. But they plainly did not, whatever their importance in certain sectors such as mining rights and government stocks. Movable goods in the form of industrial capital, personal wealth, and trading balances were overwhelmingly owned by the broad mass of the middle class. On them, primarily, depended the viability and growth of the national economy; and on them too depended the social flexibility and stability which were so much admired by foreigners.

The middle class or 'middling sort' was not, of course, a socially self-conscious or particularly coherent grouping. It remained diverse in point of both wealth and activity. A considerable distance stretched between the city bosses with great mercantile fortunes who ruled the capital, and the small tradesmen or craftsmen who represented the backbone of commercial England—the new 'nation of shopkeepers', a phrase often attributed to Napoleon at the end of the century but in fact used by Adam Smith considerably earlier. Nor was there necessarily much resemblance between the middling countryman, a substantial tenant farmer soon to be dignified perhaps by the title of gentleman farmer, and his urban counterparts, the business man, doctor, and lawyer, who throve on early industrial society. None the less, such men had much in common. Frequently self-made and always dependent on aggressive use of their talents, they were genuine 'capitalists' in terms of the investment of their labour and their profits in entrepreneurial activity, whether commercial or professional. Together they owned, controlled, or operated the most dynamic portions of the economy. Politically, their supremacy was rarely challenged in towns of any size, and even in many rural parishes they more nearly represented the ruling class than the lofty oligarchs and lordly magnates who seemed so important at Whitehall and Westminster.

Everywhere the dominant tone of this class, with its pragmatic attitudes and its frankly commercial logic, was discernible. Not least was its influence apparent in education, a matter in which the eighteenth century has acquired a wretched reputation. Inspection of the great institutions of the Tudor and Stuart academic world, the grammar schools and the universities, is not reassuring in this respect. Grammar schools which continued vigorously to fulfil their function of offering a scholarly education to relatively humble children were few indeed. Most endowments proved inadequate to sustain the expenses or escape the cupidity of those who controlled them. The clergy who taught in them frequently did their best but rarely surmounted the discouraging effects of low salaries and poor support. The universities in England gave an impression of complacency and sloth, particularly by comparison with their Scottish counterparts. North of the border, academic life was characterized by religious strife and even bigotry. But it also displayed signs of immense vigour on which the Scottish Enlightenment prospered. The Scottish contribution to the European achievement of the age in fields as diverse as moral philosophy, political economy, and medical science was substantial. The English universities fell far short by this yardstick. Their function was partly to train their clergy, partly to offer a broad education to the genteel and the wealthy. This they performed with more zest than they are generally allowed. The disciplined and innovative instruction offered at a new foundation like Hertford in Oxford, or the genuine progress of mathematical scholarship at Cambridge by no means confirm the impression given by Rowlandson prints or anti-clerical propaganda. Even so, they plainly did not meet the demands of the middle class.

But the fact was that they were not expected to. In default of the grammar schools and the universities, the characteristically middle-class devices of subscription and fees were bringing into existence a great mass of practical, progressive education designed to fit the sons of the middling sort to staff the professions and the world of business. These schools were often short-lived, and when they passed they left so little behind them that it was easy for censorious Victorians to assume that they had never existed. Even the greatest of the eighteenth-century schools, including dissenting academies like those at Northampton and Warrington, among the best of their kind, withered before very long. But in the mean time they offered exactly the basic, unpretentious education on which the business classes depended.

The result was emphatically a middle-class culture, with an unmistakably pragmatic tone. If there was an English Enlightenment it was perhaps in this sense, an enlightenment of the practical mind. The fascination of the mid-eighteenth century was neither with theological polemics nor with philosophical speculation, but rather with applied technology. The Society of Arts, founded in 1758, was an appropriate expression of this spirit. Perhaps its most controversial project during its early years was a scheme to bring fish from the coast to London by road, thereby breaking the monopoly of the Thames fish dealers, and dramatically lowering the price of a valuable and (it was stressed) a nutritious commodity. It was faintly bizarre, no doubt, but its object was pre-eminently practical. The Society of Arts was a great national concern, but it was only the most famous of many formal and informal, enduring and ephemeral, clubs and associations which fed on the interest in scientific or pseudo-scientific knowledge. Such interest was at least as enthusiastic in the provinces as in the metropolis. Again, the Lichfield circle associated with Erasmus Darwin and the Lunar Society were only the most celebrated of many amateur groups with very earnest attitudes. The stream of literature which they helped to generate also provides a rough index to the growth of popular interest in matters scientific. Even the monthly magazines, designed primarily with a view to entertainment, featured the myriad inventions and speculations of an age deeply committed to the exploration of the physical world.

Middle-class work and study required middle-class play and diversions. The eighteenth century will for ever be associated with the amusements of a fashionable oligarchical society, represented most notably in the prime of the first of the great spa towns. Yet Bath would have been a shadow of its Georgian self without its middle-class clientele. The enterprise of the Woods as developers and of 'Beau' Nash as the first master of ceremonies was dependent not merely on the names of the great but also on the money of the middling. For every nobleman reported as taking the waters or attending the Assembly, there had to be a host of those paying for a share in the genteel atmosphere which was created. In this respect, as in so many others, it was the constant fidelity of the middling sort to the fashions and habits of their social superiors which sustained the commercial viability of leisure and luxury while maintaining the impression of a dominant and patronizing aristocratic élite. Bath, in any case, was hardly unique. The spas were after all a regional as well as a national phenomenon, offering in the provinces a number of fair imitations of their more celebrated model. When Daniel Defoe toured England in the early 1720s he discovered many spa towns. Tunbridge, he noted with surprise, was a town in which 'company and diversion is the main business of the place'. But Tunbridge had several competitors around the capital: Epsom, Dulwich, and Sydenham Wells all provided attractive resorts for Londoners seeking country air and mineral salts. In the Peak District, already a favourite area for the ancestor of the modern tourist, he found the demands of visitors outstripping the available accommodation at Buxton and Matlock. Buxton, especially, was to grow rapidly in the mid-eighteenth century, though by the 1780s its own rivalry with Tunbridge for second place to Bath was under pressure from a newcomer, Cheltenham.

Spa water, of course, was in limited supply, but there was no shortage of another valuable commodity, sea water. In this as in the case of the spas, the appropriate combination of health and recreation was provided by the co-operation of the medical profession, which hastened to testify to the inestimable benefits of salt water and sea air. Brighton was not developed to any extent until the 1790s. But the development of seaside resorts had begun long before. Dr Russell's *A Dissertation on the Use of Sea Water in the Diseases of the Glands*, published in 1749, was an important influence in this process. Weymouth, which made much of the high proportion of minerals in the waters of the English Channel, was already a flourishing resort by 1780. Margate and Ramsgate with easy access from London had established themselves even earlier, and offered more sophisticated and varied arrangements. Scarborough on the Yorkshire coast was equally advanced. The medical element in these developments was certainly important. But it is difficult not to see the essential impetus as deriving from more mundane social needs. Between fashionable society with its ritual divisions of the years and its court-orientated timetables, and the despised fairs and holidays of the lower sort, there was a considerable gap, a gap which the new resorts filled with immense success and profit. They were essentially middle-class, urban living transported temporarily to new surroundings, the bourgeois equivalent of the aristocrat's retreat to country-house life. Their underlying basis was the generally felt need for distinctively middle-class recreations. The use of fees or subscriptions ensured respectable company and a decently moneyed atmosphere. Particularly for women, in some ways the most obvious beneficiaries of the new affluence, such a flexible, yet protected environment was crucial. Long before the emergence of the resorts, its character had been fully displayed in what Defoe called the 'new fashion'd way of conversing by assemblies'. Assemblies, providing dancing, cards, tea-drinking, and general social mixing, were commonplace by the middle of the century. Even in many market towns they provided an invaluable focus for activities as businesslike as the marriage market, and as casual as country gossip. In the largest cities, spectacular displays of civic pride could be involved; at Norwich the theatre and the assembly hall erected in the 1750s featured striking designs by the local architect, Thomas Ivory. They went up at much the same time as a magnificent new dissenting church, a not inappropriate demonstration of the social link between religion and recreation. Many of those who paid for their admission to the almost daily 'routs' in the Assembly also made their way on Sunday to the chapel.

To force all the cultural developments of a complex age into a single pattern might seem incautious. Yet there is little doubt that the dominating tone of the mid-Georgian arts closely corresponded to the needs of a large, wealthy, and pretentious middle class. There was no simple retreat from austere aristocratic classicism to bourgeois romanticism. Rather the classical tradition continued to be interpreted as it had been for generations since the Renaissance. But about the ubiquitous Adam fireplaces and Wedgwood pottery there was a distinctly new and even anti-aristocratic spirit. The triumphs of the Augustan arts had been the triumphs of an élite, intended primarily for the consumption of an élite. Order, structure, and form were the hallmarks of early eighteenth-century art and a sophisticated sense of their classical significance the key to interpreting them. The Horatian satires of a Pope, the Palladian designs of a Burlington, and the still essentially formal landscape gardening beloved of classicists such as William Kent, belonged to the same world. But twenty years later few pragmatic products of a middle-class education would have appreciated the linguistic nuances of a satire and fewer still would have understood or identified with the Venetian Renaissance. By contrast the cultural achievements of the mid-century required neither sophistication nor subtlety. The picturesque gardening publicized by William Shenstone, and still more the vogue for 'natural' landscaping exploited by 'Capability' Brown, represented a major break with the early eighteenth-century passion for classical imitation and allusion. This was also markedly true of the new literary developments. The specifically bourgeois nature of the novel, whether in its picaresque or puritanical form, needs little emphasis. Sometimes, as in Richardson's jaundiced portrayal of rakish aristocrats in *Pamela* and *Clarissa* it was almost painfully prominent. At other times, as in the adventure stories of Smollett and Fielding, it took the form of a moralistic interest in the social life of the lower and middling sort. In any event these trends came together and produced their most characteristic expression in the triumph of sentiment in the 1760s. Laurence Sterne's *Tristram Shandy*, for example, invaded the palace as well as the parlour, and appealed to the plutocrat as well as the tradesman. But the widespread enthusiasm for the sentimental movement should not be allowed to obscure its significance as a vehicle of middle-class values and attitudes. Sentiment consummated in fantasy what the wealth of commercial England was bringing nearer in reality, the acquisition of gentility by a consumer society. Sentiment made 'natural' taste, the taste of the virtuous man, regardless of upbringing or breeding, the true criterion of gentility; it also boosted the domestic morality of the middle class with its stress on family life and its devotion to Calvinistic conceptions of virtue, against heroic but hierarchical notions of personal honour. After George II's death in 1760, the new king and queen were to prove altogether appropriate emblems of such ideals, giving to court society an air which can seem almost Victorian. In this, they faithfully reflected the mores of many of their subjects. Earlier middle classes had merely aped their social betters. Now there was, in theory at least, no need for aping them. Manners in this Brave New World needed no acquiring and a Man of Feeling, like the hero of Mackenzie's influential work of that name, was effectively classless.

If a middle-class culture was sentimental it was also marked by a certain insularity, tempered only by the anxiety of artists themselves to demonstrate their openness to external influences. But activities of intellectual trend-setters in this respect could be somewhat misleading. Sir Joshua Reynolds, the recognized maestro of English art in the new reign, consciously appealed to Continental models, and saw himself transmitting to a vulgar but expectant public superior traditions of European art. Yet in a way he embodied many of the new trends at home. For Reynolds, like his colleagues Hayman and Gainsborough, depended as much on a newly moneyed public as on more aristocratic patrons. In a way too, his influence neatly reflected both the national vitality and organized professionalism characteristic of the period. The emergence of the Royal Academy in 1768 saw at one level a representative association comparable to the professional bodies which were beginning to appear on behalf of doctors and lawyers. At another level it brought to a peak a vigorous native art such as Hogarth had heralded but never seen. Not that foreign influences were unimportant in this or in other fields of cultural endeavour. Angelica Kauffmann was the most sought-after decorator of fashionable London, Johann Zoffany one of its most successful portraitists. But neither played the part that foreigners had earlier in the century. There was no Verrio dominating the art of grand decoration, no Handel towering over English musicians, no Rysbrack or Roubiliac leading the way in monumental sculpture. Instead, there were the Adams to embellish the Englishman's house, a Burney or Boyce to educate his ear, a Wilton to commemorate his passing.

The new cultural confidence was nowhere more marked than among the painters themselves. What had been most striking about Hogarth's self-conscious attempts to create a truly native tradition had been his isolation in this grand enterprise. What was striking about his successors of the English school was the ease with which they felt free to appropriate Continental techniques without a sense of inferiority or dependence. In this respect Joseph Wright of Derby, not the most praised but perhaps the most innovative of mid-century artists, was also thoroughly representative. Appropriately he was a friend of Erasmus Darwin, grandfather of Charles and himself a distinguished physician, scientist, and even poet. Wright was at his best with his semi-educational studies of scientific experiments and discoveries. But he was also the skilled manipulator of light in ways which would not have shamed Caravaggio. Like everyone, Wright went to Italy, but after his major masterpieces not before; when he returned he seemed to many to have lost rather than gained inspiration.

The Politics of Protest

The social changes which made their mark on mid-Georgian England were profound, extensive, and of the utmost consequence for the future. But their immediate impact on the political structure, at a time when the power of prescription and force of custom were overriding, is difficult to assess. Superficially there were few changes in the character of politics around the middle of the century. The administrations of North (1770–82) and the younger Pitt (1783–1801) were to provoke comparisons in point of both technique and policy with those of Walpole and Pelham. Of great constitutional changes there were few indeed; the torrent of agitation and reform which threatened the *ancien régime* in the nineteenth century seems in retrospect an unconscionable time arriving. Yet appearances in this respect were deeply deceptive. The language, the objectives, even the mechanics of politics were all influenced by awareness of a large political nation which lay beyond the immediate world of Whitehall and Westminster. If nothing else the extent and bitterness of the polemical warfare which occurred in newspapers, prints, and pamphlets in the 1750s and 1760s would be adequate testimony to the vitality of public debate and the concern of politicians to engage in it. In this debate, one of the latter seemed to occupy a special place. The elder Pitt's reputation is such that, even after two centuries, it is difficult to give him the critical treatment which such an influential figure requires. Before 1754 Pitt's career had been far from an unqualified success. The younger son in a spendthrift and eccentric family, Pitt had joined and eventually married into one of the great Whig houses, that of Temple of Stowe. As a young man he made his political name as a patriot orator of fearsome rhetoric and imprudent vehemence. His anti-Hanoverian outbursts during the War of the Austrian Succession acquired widespread publicity and earned him useful popularity, but they rendered him almost permanently *persona non grata* with the king. When, in 1746, the Pelhams were able to offer him office it was on terms which provided profit without prospects. As Paymaster-General, Pitt was excluded from the making of high policy and effectively muzzled in parliamentary debate. It seemed yet another example of a patriot's progress, sacrificing principle to promotion. But Pitt's fortunes were dramatically changed by the events of the mid-1750s. The sudden death of Henry Pelham in 1754 seemed even at the time a watershed, indicated not least by the king's own observation on its significance: 'Now I shall have no more peace.' Pelham's successor was his brother, Newcastle, a shrewd, experienced minister, and by no means the ridiculous mediocrity portrayed by Whig legend. But in the Lords he found it difficult to exercise the controlling influence either of his brother or of Walpole. Pitt's principal rival in the Commons, Henry Fox, lacked the political courage or weight to replace Pelham. The 'old corps' of Whigs, the dominant force in Parliament since the Hanoverian accession, was almost without leadership. Their Tory opponents, by now increasingly restive under continuing proscription and no longer disposed to think seriously of a king over the water, also sought inspiration. Could not Pitt provide what both needed?

That he was able to do so owed much to circumstance, and in particular to the international situation. The War of Austrian Succession had identified major areas of conflict for the future without beginning to settle them. The principal focus overseas was no longer the fate of the Spanish Empire, but the world-wide conflict threatening between Britain and France, in a mercantilist age the most successful mercantilist powers. In North America, the French sought to forge a chain from Quebec to Louisiana, cutting off the English colonies. In the West Indies there was constant bickering over disputed sugar islands, as there was in West Africa over the trade in slaves and gum. In India the factiousness and feebleness of native princes combined with the rapacity of the French and English East India Companies to create a highly volatile situation. Everything pointed to a desperate and conclusive war for empire. When it came it began disastrously both for England and for Pitt's political rivals. In 1755–6, failure to deal the French navy a decisive blow in the Atlantic, and the loss of Minorca in the Mediterranean, if anything heightened by the ruthlessness with which the hapless Admiral Byng was sacrificed, left the old Whig regime discredited if not devastated. This was the making of Pitt, and perhaps of the First British Empire.

The ensuing years have taken their place in history as a period of exceptional importance and exceptional achievement. The successes of the Seven Years War, which decisively defeated France in North America and India, and turned back the Bourbon threat elsewhere, represented a high point of imperial achievement and made Pitt the most gloriously successful war minister in British history. Moreover, his triumph in trouncing the 'old corps' politicians seemed to suggest a new kind of politician and a new kind of politics, neatly encapsulated in Dr Johnson's contrast between Walpole as a 'minister given by the king to the people', and Pitt as a 'minister given by the people to the king'. Yet Pitt made his way to power more by shrewd political judgement and sheer luck than by public acclaim. His supposedly popular support was engineered by his friends in the City of London and by his new-found Tory associates in the provinces. His first essay in power, the Pitt–Devonshire ministry of 1756–7, was weak and short-lived; his second, the coalition of 1757, was much more successful, thanks partly to a deal with Newcastle, partly to the support of the Prince of Wales, the future George III. This combination of the reversionary interest and the 'old corps' was as cynical an exercise in political manœuvre as anything conceived by Pitt's predecessors and opponents; it corresponded closely with what Walpole had done in 1720 when he and Prince George (the later George II) had bullied and wheedled their way back to court.

Nor did the war quite present the unblemished record which Pitt's admirers were to make of it. The fundamental strategy which Pitt pursued was completely at variance with the patriot programme which he had previously espoused. His commitment to an expensive alliance with Prussia and his generous deployment of British resources both in money and men to maintain an army in Germany followed naturally from the diplomatic strategy of Pelham and Newcastle. Pitt's own most characteristic contribution to the war, his use of combined operations against the coast of France, designed to divert French attention from the war in Germany, was a desperate attempt to prove his patriot credentials to his friends the Tories, already increasingly dismayed by his 'Hanoverian' policies. In military terms, they were wasteful and largely ineffective. When victory eventually came, it owed much to forces over which Pitt had little control. In general, the French paid heavily for their failure to build up resources for naval and colonial warfare. In India, the advantage enjoyed by the British East India Company was marginal but it was decisive, particularly when the talents of Clive were thrown into the balance. Pitt's description of Clive as a 'heaven-born' general was a rhetorical admission that he could not claim the credit for Clive's appointment himself. Even Wolfe, whose heroic assault on Quebec captured the national imagination, was only the last of a number of commanders whose activities in North America by no means achieved uniform success. But victory solves all problems in war, at least until a peace has to be negotiated. Before the *annus mirabilis* of 1759, when the tide turned both in the West Indies and in North America, Pitt's coalition with Newcastle was precariously balanced on the brink of disintegration. Pitt's Tory supporters constantly talked of deserting a minister whose policies filled them with alarm, while his ally Newcastle repeatedly threatened to ditch a colleague who spent money like water in pursuit of costly defeats. In 1759 these difficulties dissolved.

Pitt did not fully deserve the credit for the fortunes of the Seven Years War but there were two important respects in which his historical reputation seems justified. For if Pitt's popular credentials have been exaggerated, his role in changing the character of eighteenth-century politics was none the less an important one. In the mid-1750s the mould was plainly cracking. The proscription of Toryism, and the ability of the Whig families to keep the control of patronage within a narrow circle, had a very short future. Pitt offered at least the hope of a break with the old politics, especially in the metropolis where his connections went deep into a genuinely popular electorate. Similarly, as a war leader he did provide one crucial quality which no rival possessed at this time, without which the war could not have been continued, let alone brought to a triumphant conclusion. Political courage, and with it a confidence which was difficult to distinguish from unthinking arrogance, gave other more competent and cautious men the moral base on which to fight and win a brilliant war. Pitt's faith in his own leadership provided a key component in the direction of the war at the very moment when the leaders of the old Whig gang,

Newcastle and Fox, had manifestly lost their nerve. If political laurels go in the last analysis to those prepared to risk everything, then in this sense at least Pitt deserved them.

Whatever the nature of Pitt's achievement, his controversial activities in these years formed a fitting prologue to the drama which was shortly to follow. The transformed character of politics in the 1760s will be for ever associated with the new king George III and with one of his most turbulent subjects, John Wilkes. So far as the king was concerned these years were to prove traumatic in the extreme. Yet much of what George III did was the logical culmination of trends in his grandfather's reign. This was particularly true of his supposedly revolutionary determination to abolish the old party distinctions. The validity of such distinctions had already been diminished by the success of Frederick Prince of Wales and Pitt in enlisting the aid of the Tories. The difference in 1760 was one of tone rather than substance with reluctant and grudging toleration being replaced by unavowed pride in the accessibility of the new regime to the old Tories. At court, they were welcomed back with open arms and with a judicious distribution of offices, honours, and peerages. In the counties, they returned, where they had not returned during the preceding decade, to the commissions of the peace; in the midland shires the commissions once again resembled a roll call of the country gentry, many of them of old Tory and even old royalist stock. One redoubtable Tory was granted a special place in the sun. Dr Johnson, the literary giant of the age, basked in the political approval of the new regime, signalized with a pension from Lord Bute in 1762. His new acceptability was not without irony. In the 1730s Johnson had written a bitter patriot attack on the pro-Spanish policy of Walpole in relation to the Caribbean, and British claims there. Now, under the new king, he was to pen an equally powerful and more compelling piece in defence of George III's supposed appeasement of Spain over the British claim to the Falkland Islands, which he described as 'a bleak and gloomy solitude, an island thrown aside from human use, stormy in winter, and barren in summer'. This was not the end of the Falkland Islands as an issue in the history of British foreign policy. What Johnson's progress as an individual signified was still more strikingly endorsed institutionally in the history of Oxford University. For forty-six years the home and shrine of sentimental Jacobitism had suffered in the political wilderness, as successive generations of Whig churchmen monopolized the places of honour and profit. The ecclesiastical masters of early Hanoverian England had generally been trained either at Cambridge or at the tiny minority of Whig colleges at Oxford. In the new reign, there was no doubt which university made its emotional home-coming. Oddly enough, Oxford had contributed more than one Prime Minister even to early Hanoverian government. But Pelham had made little attempt to prevent his brother's direction of ecclesiastical patronage to Cambridge, and Pitt had at one time stooped to making capital of his own university's Jacobite associations. Under George. III, Oxford was to have in Lord North a Prime Minister who was also its Chancellor, and one who fittingly represented the old Tory families of the cavalier counties.

If the return to court of the Tories was unsurprising, George III's other new measures seem hardly less so. The reign began in a haze of good intentions and lofty aspirations. Any notion that a new 'patriot king' might seek to strengthen the royal prerogative was quickly crushed. The Demise of the Crown Act, which stipulated that judges would not as in the past resign their offices at the death of the sovereign, removed any suspicion that kings might use their legal rights to sweep away the Whig judicial establishment. At the same time, the Civil List Act provided for a strictly controlled royal allowance of £800,000 per annum; this was the same as that granted to George II but there was the important additional provision that any surplus produced by the civil list duties was for the future directed to the Exchequer not to the Crown. With inflation, this stipulation was seriously to impede the Crown's capacity to cope with the rising tide of court expenses and ironically proved to be a most damaging concession by the king in the name of patriotic propriety. This was the true legacy of the Leicester House party under Frederick Prince of Wales—not a fanciful scheme for the creation of a new benevolent despotism, but further limitation of the Crown's prerogative.

These, however, were minor matters compared with the most important of the new regime's priorities—peace. The old ministers, Pitt and Newcastle, both resigned from office, the former in 1761 because George III and Bute declined to extend the war to Spain at his insistence, the latter specifically in protest against the peace terms the next year. But most of the arguments which they deployed carry little weight in retrospect. Peace could not be secured without restoring to the Bourbons a proportion of the gains made during the war. The return of the principal French West Indian Islands and the preservation of French fishing rights in Canadian waters were not excessive concessions, nor would Pitt and Newcastle, in the diplomatic circumstances of 1762, have been able to make less without continuing the war to the bitter end. Moreover the immense successes of recent years had been gained at a fearful financial cost, which by 1761 was provoking widespread alarm. The case against further prosecution of the war, put repeatedly in newspapers and pamphlets and led by Israel Mauduit's *Considerations on the German War*, was a strong one. War *à outrance* would end in bankruptcy; moreover its object—continued support of Frederick the Great and the acquisition of some additional colonial possessions—seemed of doubtful value. It is possible that George III and Bute, moved in part by the reflection that the war, for all its glory, was not their war, and influenced also by the need to make a quick peace, surrendered rather more than they needed to, particularly in the terms they made with Spain. But in essentials their peace was a prudent, defensible measure and was overwhelmingly approved by parliamentary and public opinion.

Why, in these circumstances, did the new reign prove so controversial? Mainly, perhaps, it was because the new men brought to their otherwise innocuous activities a degree of personal animosity towards the old regime which was bound to cause difficulties. The chosen instrument of George III's reforms was his former tutor, Lord Bute, a Scottish peer of intellectual bent whose experience and skills were slight. Most of the instruction with which he had prepared the young king for his task was more naïve than knavish. There was no great conspiracy against liberty and the constitution, nor any determination to introduce a new authoritarian system. But there was undoubtedly on the part of the new king and his minister a deep-seated resentment of the men who had monopolized power under George II and a readiness if not a determination to dispense with, even to humiliate them. For 'black-hearted' Pitt, who was seen as betraying the prince's court in 1757, there was outright hatred, and it is difficult to see how Pitt and Bute could have co-operated in the new circumstances. But Pitt was a megalomaniac with whom only a saint could have co-operated for long. The great Whig families were another matter. Their rank, weight, and inherited importance would make them dangerous enemies. No doubt they treated the new king with a measure of condescension. Families such as the Cavendishes were apt to regard themselves as kingmakers, for whom the electors of Hanover were at most *primi inter pares*. Newcastle, after a lifetime in office, might be forgiven for expecting to have his advice taken seriously by a donnish, ineffectual Scottish peer who was chiefly known for the shapeliness of his legs and his patronage of botanists. There were, in short, good reasons for proceeding cautiously, and above all reasons for ensuring as smooth a transition as possible between the new and the old politics. This was by no means out of the question. The 'old corps' Whigs knew well that the substance of Bute's demands must be granted. Most of them, in the absence of a charismatic leader of their own, were content to labour on under changed management. A typical figure was Lord North, himself a cousin of the duke of Newcastle, a future Prime Minister and in the new reign a passive adherent of George III's court. Even the senior men, who saw themselves as victims of the new order, were reluctant to declare war on it. Hardwicke, the doyen of Whig lawyers and one of the pillars of the Pelhamite system, sought only dignified provision for his friends and a continuing supply of places at court for his family. Given this background, it was maladroit of Bute and George III to drive out Newcastle and his friends. When they did so, ostensibly over the peace terms in the spring of 1762, they created one of the most enduring enmities in modern British politics.

Perhaps the alienation of the old political establishment would have been a price worth paying if the new plans had worked out. But Bute himself, having beset his young charge with powerful enemies, chose to resign from office after only a year, with the lordly intention of directing affairs from the back-benches, or rather (as it was inevitably seen) from the backstairs. And so to the folly of antagonizing the old Whig families was added that of providing them with a legend of intrigue and influence with which to sustain and inspire their opposition. This opposition and the equivocal conduct of Bute set the pattern for twenty years or more of politics. In the short run, the 1760s featured a nightmarish cycle of ministerial instability, as George III sought a minister who was both congenial in the closet and capable of presiding in Parliament. In the process, the Whigs themselves under Lord Rockingham, Pitt, and the duke of Grafton were tried and found wanting, until in 1770 Lord North emerged as a figure capable of wearing the mantle of Walpole and Pelham. Running through these years of tortuous, factious politics there was always the *damnosa hereditas* of Bute's inconsequential yet damaging flirtation with power, the suspicion of the Whig families, and the myth of a continuing improper secret influence. When Edmund Burke produced his comprehensive and classic analysis of the politics of the period, *Thoughts on the Cause of the Present Discontents* (1770), it was this influence which gave him the basis for a systematic onslaught on the new court and its system. The *Thoughts* were to pass into history as the authorized version of the Whig party, and for many later generations the standard account of the misdeeds of George III.

There was other inflammable material at hand in the 1760s. The war was succeeded by a serious economic slump which clearly demonstrates the uneven distribution of economic rewards in the age of enterprise. The period was marked by a series of violent industrial disputes which created widespread unrest in urban centres such as Manchester and Newcastle, and threatened to spill over into political agitation. Even in the countryside these were years of bad harvests, rising prices, and serious dearth. In this atmosphere the activities of John Wilkes found ample support. Wilkes's historical reputation as an amiable rogue has, to some extent, obscured his political shrewdness and inventiveness. Circumstances and opportunism were the making of Wilkes. The grievances which he took up would have made little impact ten years earlier. The general warrants, which permitted arbitrary arrest for political offences, and which caused so much controversy when Wilkes's journalistic activities provoked George III's ministers to deploy them, had been a familiar feature of Hanoverian government. They were used, for example, by both Pitt and Newcastle in their time. But then they had been justified by reference to the Jacobite threat, and they had been used against proscribed Tories rather than vociferous Whigs. Similarly when, in 1768, Wilkes stood for the county of Middlesex and found himself barred from his seat in the Commons there were tolerable precedents and adequate legal arguments for his exclusion. But the Middlesex election involved a popular county intimately connected with the feverish politics of the capital; the Middlesex electors could not be treated as if they were a handful of voters in a rotten borough. Three years later, when Wilkes and his friends attacked the right of the House of Commons to prevent the public reporting of its debates, they were attacking an old and jealously guarded privilege of the legislature. But the defence of that privilege proved hopelessly impracticable in the new climate. The Wilkesite radicals were typically small businessmen, craftsmen, and artisans. They represented the 'middling and inferior sort' at its most concentrated, its most articulate, and its most volatile.

When they took their grievance to the country they found support not only among provincial gentlemen worried by the threat to electoral rights but also among their own counterparts in towns up and down the country. The middle class, the crucial element in their campaign, had no unified politics, and protest was not necessarily their preferred political role. But their part in the Wilkesite movement unmistakably signalized their novel importance in the politics of George III's reign. Yet this importance was only in part of their own making. The rules by which the political game had been played under the early Hanoverians no longer applied, whatever precedents they offered; for the men who had found them advantageous now found it convenient to abandon them. The old Whigs, by their readiness to use any weapon of revenge against George III, did much to legitimize the new spirit of popular opposition to the court. Without this collaboration from highly respectable elements in the ruling class, the popular convulsions associated with Wilkes would have been a matter of much less consequence.

Rebellion and Reform

The early years of the new reign have always attracted attention for their colourful politics. Yet in some ways the most striking changes of the period concerned Britain's role overseas, especially the new awareness of empire which inevitably succeeded the Seven Years War. The effective hegemony of North America was especially entrancing. Imperial civil servants and ministers enjoyed a brief period of uninhibited inventiveness in the early 1760s as they planned a new and rosy future for the transatlantic colonies. Quebec was to provide a veritable cornucopia of fish and fur. The American colonies, reinforced by settlement in Canada and the Floridas, would form a vast, loyal market for British manufactures, a continuing source of essential raw materials, and even (enticing prospect for a debt-ridden mother country) a new source of revenue for the Treasury. The

West Indies, firmly entrenched in a more effectively policed mercantilist system, would maximize the benefits of a flourishing slave trade, provide a steady flow of tropical products, and form a valuable base for commercial incursions into the Spanish Empire. In the East still more speculative and still more exciting prospects appeared. After Clive's victory at Plassey in 1757 Britain had emerged as the dominant European power on the subcontinent. There was, technically, no territorial presence in the East Indies, but in reality from this time the British East India Company was inextricably involved in effective colonization. In this respect 1765, when Clive formally accepted the *diwani* (land revenues) of Bengal on behalf of the company and thereby committed it to direct political control rather than mere commercial activity, was a landmark as important as Plassey itself, though it followed logically from it. These events transformed the British perception of India. The exotic character of the new possessions and the fact that they brought to light a previously unappreciated culture made the impact of the new empire particularly powerful. This impact was early expressed by Francis Hayman's massive portrayal of Clive receiving the submission of native princes, erected at that pantheon of genteel amusements, Ranelagh, in 1765. Imports of Asian curiosities soared and for the first time something like an informed and genuine interest in Indian society began to take shape. Other aspects of the new acquisitions in the East were less refined and less affecting. In the general election of 1768, a noticeable feature of press reporting was the appearance in a number of constituencies of men who had returned from service in the East India Company and were using their allegedly ill-gotten wealth to buy their way into Parliament. The 'nabobs' had arrived. Their influence was invariably exaggerated, as were their misdeeds and villainies. Moreover, in principle they were no different from the West India planters, the 'Turkey merchants', the 'monied men', and others whose unconventional profits had incurred the enmity of older less 'diversified' families. But their appearance was inevitably a matter of intense curiosity and eventually concern. Clive himself was the embodiment of the rapacious 'nabob'; the ruthlessness and unashamedness with which he had acquired personal riches while in the service of the company seemed all too representative of an entire class of men who saw empire as the means to a fast and even felonious fortune. Nor, it seemed, were temptations restricted to India. The furious speculation in East India stock which followed the grant of the *diwani*, the consequent recurrent crises in the Company's financial affairs, and not least the government's growing interest in its activities all brought the complex and frequently corrupt character of East India politics into an unwelcome and glaring light.

America had no nabobs, but the economic and political problems caused by the preservation and extension of the American empire were greater even than the results of Eastern expansion, and their ramifications still wider. British ministers saw all too clearly the potential value of their transatlantic subjects, but they did not appreciate the extent to which the thirteen colonies had developed a highly independent attitude when it came to intervention from London. Nor did they grasp the capacity of a distant, wealthy, and resourceful population of some two and a half millions to obstruct and resist imperial power. The result was a decade of cyclical crisis in Anglo-American relations, beginning with the Stamp Act, which raised the American cry of 'no taxation without representation' in 1765, and finally culminating in rebellion and war in 1775. It is not easy to identify what, in the last analysis, was at issue from the British standpoint, even at two centuries' distance. By 1775 most of the aims of the post-war ministers had been explicitly or tacitly abandoned. Not even the most optimistic can have thought by 1775 that America was going to prove what Lord Rockingham called a 'revenue mine'. Quelling the colonies by force was bound to be as expensive as its ultimate consequences were bound to be unpredictable. European enemies would plainly see the War of Independence as an opportunity to redress that balance which had tilted so much to their disadvantage in the Seven Years War. Moreover there were those who challenged the entire basis of the war as a logical conclusion from mercantilist principles. Adam Smith's *Wealth of Nations*, published in the same year as the Declaration of Independence (and incidentally at the same time as the first volume of Edward Gibbon's pessimistic survey of the Roman Empire) systematically demolished the economic case for empire. Yet with a few exceptions, notably the radical politicians of the metropolis and some of the religious dissenters, Englishmen strongly supported the war against America. Its central principle, the defence of unlimited parliamentary sovereignty, was naturally important in this, the great age of that principle. William Blackstone's celebrated *Commentaries on the Laws of England*, published in 1765, had announced with uncompromising clarity the unbounded legal authority of the Crown-in-Parliament; the conflict with America was its clearest possible expression. Moreover, the economic arguments which seem so attractive in retrospect made little impression when they were first put. For most Englishmen the only viable concept of empire was the old mercantilist one. Colonies which declined to accept the full extent of parliamentary supremacy were not merely worthless, they were positively dangerous. Against this belief that an empire out of control was worse than no empire at all, more imaginative minds made little progress. Here, if ever, there was a clash of chronology and culture. Americans at heart were defending the rights of seventeenth-century Englishmen. For them, resistance to the stamp tax was on a par with Hampden's struggle against ship money; a sovereignty which overrode provincial assemblies and local rights was unthinkable. Englishmen, on the other hand, were deploying an eighteenth-century weapon, parliamentary supremacy, in what was one of the eighteenth century's most cherished doctrines, the indivisible and unlimited authority of metropolitan power in a mercantilist system. Only force would decide the outcome.

In due course, the outcome was determined in favour of the new United States. In the interim the war proved a disaster for

Britain—worse by far than anything since the Second Dutch War of 1665–7. It grew from being a colonial insurgency to an all-out war against the Bourbon monarchies, and eventually involved hostilities with the Dutch and a state of 'armed neutrality' with other powers. At the peace negotiations of 1782–3 a certain amount was saved from the wreckage. Although the thirteen colonies were lost irretrievably, a brilliant naval victory at 'the Saints' by Admiral Rodney in 1782 preserved the British West Indies and above all saved George III the embarrassment of surrendering what Cromwell had gained over a century before, the much-prized jewel of Jamaica. In the Mediterranean, Spain's attempt at the reconquest of Gibraltar was foiled. In India, Warren Hastings's desperate defence of Clive's acquisitions staved off both French *revanche* and princely rebellion. Contemporaries found the independence of America a bitter pill to swallow, but most of the empire outside the thirteen colonies remained intact, and at least the utter humiliation feared in the darkest days of the war was averted.

Almost more important than the overseas consequences of the American War were the domestic implications. The economic problems caused to a nascent industrial society by a world war and the accompanying embargoes on trade were immense. In the ensuing recession both the stock market and land values plunged to alarmingly low levels, unseen in many years. Unprecedentedly high taxes and the rapid growth of the National Debt reinforced the financial crisis and created serious economic problems. Fundamental questions were raised about government, Parliament, and the political system generally. In the ensuing chaos, relatively conservative forces, not least the country gentry, were swept into what looked like an open attack on the constitution, with the Association movement of 1779–80. The Associations had widespread support in the counties, the capital, and provincial cities, and in their demands for reform went further than all but the wilder radicals of the Wilkesite movement. Christopher Wyvill, the Yorkshire cleric and country gentleman, who came close to exercising national leadership of the movement, was hardly himself such a radical. Yet his

demands for the elimination of rotten boroughs, the extension
of the franchise, and the introduction of the secret ballot, had a
futuristic ring about them. Moreover, there was about the
Associations a hint, or in the mouths of metropolitan agitators
such as John Jebb and Major Cartwright, a definite suggestion,
that Parliament, if it resisted reform, should be superseded by
the delegates of the counties. Contemporary fears of this new
phenomenon were unnecessarily colourful. Yet in retrospect it
is difficult not to be struck by the vigour and extent of the
Association movement. It arguably brought reform nearer than
at any time in the ensuing fifty years, and at its height in 1780 it
achieved an extraordinary degree of national consensus. At this
point even the House of Commons, notwithstanding the weight
of vested interests in and out of government, passed a resolu-
tion declaring that the 'influence of the crown has increased, is
increasing and ought to be diminished'. This was the signal for
almost five years of intense political controversy and sustained
ideological conflict.

Why, then, did the Association movement fail to fulfil its
promise? When Lord North gave way to a brief period of Whig
rule in 1782 Burke and his colleagues pushed through Parliament a handful of reforms abolishing some of the more
notorious sinecure places and providing for a more intensive
scrutiny of Crown finances. But parliamentary reform proved
elusive. Even when the younger Pitt was granted supreme
power in 1784 and reform was actually proposed from the
Treasury bench with the Prime Minister's authority, there was
nothing like a parliamentary majority for it. In large measure
this had to do with the circumstances in which the Association
movement was born. Genuine enthusiasm for root and branch
reform was limited, and generally confined to the articulate and
the urban. It sometimes made a disproportionately loud noise
but real support even among the urban bourgeoisie was restricted. Association sprang from a national crisis in which any
systematic critique of the existing politics would prove attractive. The outcry of the reformers against the waste and ineffici-

ency of the court system seemed particularly appropriate. The same phenomenon was to appear for the same reason thirty years later when the immense expenditure of the Napoleonic Wars and the economic crisis associated with it produced similar protests. But these conditions were short-lived and most of the interest in reform died with them. By the mid-1780s there was a growing sense of commercial revival and financial recovery, not least due to the impact of the younger Pitt's policies. Prosperity removed the stimulus to reform more effectively than any argument could.

An additional consideration was the wide and growing concern at the measures of the extremists. The lunatic fringe of the reform movement seemed to be challenging not merely the corrupt politics of the court, but the constitutional framework which supported it, and even the propertied order itself. What was to become the 'Rights of Man' school was already visible in the writings of the early reform movement. Men such as Richard Price and Joseph Priestley were, by the standards of a later age, moderate enough. But they were challenging some of the most entrenched attitudes and commonplace ideas of their day and it needed very little to force apart their fragile alliance with backwoods gentry and provincial business men. In this context the Gordon Riots proved particularly damaging. There was no direct connection between the reformers and the Gordon rioters, who held London at their mercy for nearly a week and engaged in an orgy of murder and destruction in the spring of 1780. Their cause was unashamed religious prejudice, their aim to repeal the liberal measure of relief for Roman Catholics which had been passed with the support of both government and opposition in 1778. As with the Jew Bill in 1754, it was clear that the legislature could easily get out of step with popular feeling. The leader of the anti-papists, Lord George Gordon, called his movement the Protestant Association, and it was easy enough for frightened men of property to make a connection between the rioters and the political activities of more respectable Associators. The conservative reaction so marked in England during the following years could be traced back in origin to this episode.

The early 1780s were not only turbulent in the extra-parliamentary sense; they also provided the same spectacle of political instability as the 1760s. This, too, was an element in the failure of reform. Before 1782 reformers in Parliament had congregated loosely around the two main Whig groups, Lord Rockingham's party and those who followed Lord Shelburne. The two wings of recognized Whiggism represented distinct traditions going back to Newcastle and the old Whig clans in the case of Rockingham, and to the elder Pitt in that of Shelburne. The most promising talent in each was also a familiar name. Charles James Fox, one of Rockingham's most radical supporters and also his most popular, was the son of that Henry Fox who had been a rival to the elder Pitt, and in the new reign briefly a tool of Lord Bute. Among Shelburne's associates was the younger Pitt—in Burke's phrase, not 'a chip off the old block' but 'the block itself'. Both were authentic reformers, both seemed to offer a fresh approach to a jaded, yet optimistic age, both held out the hope of leadership against the discredited politics of the men who had mismanaged the American War. Unfortunately, if perhaps inevitably, they turned out to be rivals rather than allies, and in the complex, bitter politics which followed Lord North's resignation in 1782, their enmity proved crucially important. The initiative was taken by Fox, who sought nothing less than total control of the Cabinet, a monopoly of power which the king detested in one whom he also found personally objectionable. Fox's weapon in the battle which followed the death of Rockingham, in the summer of 1782, was an unholy alliance with his old enemy, North. It was a deeply offensive and widely despised alliance, but the prize, control of the Commons and, therefore, as Fox saw it, of the government, seemed big enough to override demands for consistency. But there were flaws in Fox's logic. His ministry, the notorious Fox–North coalition, was short-lived. It was strongly opposed by the king himself, who systematically plotted its destruction, and also by Pitt, who wanted no dependence on

Fox and cordially detested North. When Fox obligingly provided an issue on which Pitt and the king might appeal to the
country, in the shape of a radical restructuring of the East India
Company, in effect he committed political suicide. George III
instructed the House of Lords to defeat the East India Bill, Pitt
was placed in power, and in the spring of 1784 a general
election was called. There could be no quarrelling with the
result. Fox was roundly defeated not only where the Treasury
could exert its influence, but also in the larger, more open
constituencies where public opinion mattered and where the
popular revulsion against him was manifest. When the dust
settled, Pitt was Prime Minister on an outstandingly secure
tenure, and the Whigs were thoroughly 'dished'. Above all,
reform, the hoped-for product of a hoped-for alliance between
Fox and Pitt against the combined forces of George III and
North, was dead—killed, it seemed, by the irresponsible antics
of Fox, that 'darling of the people'.

Perhaps reform was dead anyway. Once he had nodded in
the direction of his youthful principles by putting a motion for
reform which he knew could not be successful without the
backing of the Crown, Pitt as Prime Minister showed little taste
for radical political activity. A reformer he proved, but not in
matters affecting the constitution in Church and State. Many of
the demands of the 'economical reformers' for a reduction in
the corruption and waste of the court were to be carried out
under Pitt. Moreover, the first, extremely hesitant steps towards
free trade were taken under his guidance, notably in the commercial treaty with France in 1787. Difficult imperial questions
were also treated with a mixture of caution and innovation.
The Irish had already, in the crisis of the American War,
demanded parliamentary independence of Westminster, and
after obtaining it in 1782 achieved a measure of home rule. Pitt
would have given Ireland commercial equality with the mother
country had the manufacturers of the Midlands and Lancashire
allowed him to do so. His failure in this respect left Anglo-Irish
relations in an equivocal and uncertain state. India was put to
rest at least as a major issue in British politics with an East

India Act which finally gave government the ultimate say in the Company's affairs, at least when they did not exclusively concern trade. In 1791 Canada, with its incursion of loyalist settlers after the American War and its intractable 'ethnic' problem in Quebec, was given a settlement which was to endure, albeit uneasily, until 1867.

In many ways, Pitt's supremacy had a very traditional appearance. He was essentially a beneficiary of the court and of the king's support. His triumph in 1784 could be made to seem as much a triumph for the Crown as anything done by a Danby or a Sunderland. The opposition to Pitt looked traditional too. Fox depended much on the heir to the throne, the future George IV, whose antics, political, financial, and sexual, were as much the despair of the king as those of any heir to the Crown before him. But in other respects Pitt and his activities reflected the transformations of recent years. His administrative and economic reforms take their place among a great host of changes in contemporary attitudes which can easily be lost behind the political conservatism of the age. That most flourishing product of the Enlightenment mind—Utility—was already in sight. Jeremy Bentham and the philosophical radicals were yet to achieve a significant breakthrough in practical politics, but the flavour which they imparted or perhaps adopted was everywhere, as was the religious influence of Evangelicalism. The reforms which really did make an impact in this period were precisely those moral, humanitarian, pragmatic 'improvements' which delighted the Evangelical mind. John Howard's famous campaign belonged to the 1770s and 1780s. His 'voyage of discovery' or 'Circumnavigation of Charity', in Burke's words, provided a powerful stimulus to the work of prison reform, freely supported by many local magistrates. The Sunday Schools sprang from the same era of earnest endeavour, as did the widespread drive to establish friendly societies supervised by the clergy. Traditional recreations of the lower classes came increasingly under the disapproving inspection of their social superiors, particularly when, like cock-fighting and bull-baiting, they involved cruelty to animals. There was also a distinct shift in attitudes towards imperial responsibility. Burke's campaign against Warren Hastings, the saviour of British India, proved intolerably protracted and eventually unsuccessful; the impeachment had little to commend it despite Hastings' apparent guilt on some of the charges. But Hastings was the victim of changing standards of public morality. What would have been tolerated in a Clive was tolerated no longer. The treatment of subject peoples was no longer a matter of indifference at home. The interest in 'uncivilized' peoples from the Red Indians to Captain Cook's South Sea islanders, like Burke's indignation on behalf of more sophisticated but equally subjugated Asians, revealed a new sensitivity, tinged with romanticism, to the plight of the victims of empire. The most notorious target of the new sensibility was, of course, the slave trade. The campaign, led by Granville Sharp in the formative years of the 1770s, and by William Wilberforce in the 1780s, was to wait many years before success. But there were victories along the way. In the case of Sommersett, 1772, a Negro slave brought by a West Indian planter to London was freed on the grounds that no law of England authorized 'so high an act of dominion as slavery'. The publicity value of this decision was out of all proportion to its legal significance, but the interest which it aroused caught the essence of the late eighteenth-century mind, with its emphasis on human equality, religious redemption, and political conservatism. For Wilberforce and his friends were staunch defenders of the establishment in Church and State, and utterly uninterested in radical politics. In this they expressed the serious-minded, Evangelical enthusiasm of the business classes of the new industrial England. For all the supposedly unrepresentative nature of the political system it was these classes which Wilberforce's friend Pitt best represented. It was also their instinct for obstinate defence of the interests of property, combined with thrusting commercial aggressiveness and unlimited moral earnestness, which was to carry the England of the younger Pitt into the era of the French Revolution.

2. Revolution and the Rule of Law
(1789–1851)

CHRISTOPHER HARVIE

Reflections on the Revolutions

IN 1881 the young Oxford historian Arnold Toynbee delivered his *Lectures on the Industrial Revolution*, and in so doing made it as distinct a 'period' of British history as the Wars of the Roses. This makes it easy, but misleading, to conceive of an 'age of the dual revolution'—political in France and industrial in Britain. But while the storming of the Bastille was obvious *fact*, industrialization was gradual and relative in its impact. It showed up only in retrospect, and notions of 'revolution' made less sense to the British, who shuddered at the word, than to the Europeans, who knew revolution at close quarters. A Frenchman was in fact the first to use the metaphor—the economist Adolphe Blanqui in 1827—and Karl Marx gave the concept general European currency after 1848.

This makes the historian's task awkward, balancing what is significant now against what was significant then. The first directs us to industrial changes, new processes developing in obscure workshops; the second reminds us how slowly the power of the pre-industrial élites ebbed, how tenacious religion proved in the scientific age. Only around 1830 were people conscious of substantial and permanent industrial change; it took another twenty years to convince even the middle class that it had all been for the better.

Should there not be a simple factual record of developments?

In theory, yes. But the age of the 'supremacy of fact' was so ever-changing and obsessively individualistic that recording and assessing facts was another matter. There was no official population Census until 1801; before then there had been real controversy about whether the population of Britain was growing or shrinking. Although the Census subsequently developed into a sophisticated implement of social analysis, covering occupations and housing conditions, this was as gradual a process as the systematic mapping of the country, carried out by the Ordnance Survey in stages between 1791 and the 1860s. The ideology of *laissez-faire* and actual government retrenchment adversely affected statistical compilation, as fewer goods or businesses were regulated or taxed. (Continental autocracies were, by comparison, enthusiastic collectors of data about their little industrial enterprises.) So controversy still rages over some elementary questions—notably about whether industrialization did the mass of the people any good.

At this point, modern politics casts its shadow. Toynbee's contemporaries agreed with Karl Marx that capitalist industrialization had, by 1848, failed to improve the condition of the working class. After 1917 Soviet Russia seemed to demonstrate a viable alternative: 'planned industrialization'. But the costs of this, in human life and liberty, soon became apparent and, with the 'developing world' in mind, liberal economists restated the case for industrialization achieved through the operation of the free market. Even in the short term, they argued, and faced with the problem of providing resources for investment, British capitalism had increased both investment and living standards. The results of this vehement dispute have been inconclusive. They have also been restricted in their geographical context, considering that British economic development had direct, and far from fortunate, effects on Ireland, India, and the Southern States of the USA.

If there are problems with statistics and context, there is also the question of consciousness. Industrialization as a concept was only germinating in the 1820s. Whatever the governing élite thought about economic doctrines, as magistrates and landowners their watchword was stability, their values were still pre-industrial. But by 1829 the trend to industrialization became, quite suddenly, unmistakable. Only eleven years after the last of Jane Austen's novels a raucous new voice pictured the 'Signs of the Times' in the *Edinburgh Review*:

We remove mountains, and make seas our smooth highway; nothing can resist us. We war with rude nature; and by our resistless engines, come off always victorious, and loaded with spoils.

Thomas Carlyle summed up, vividly and emotionally, a plethora of contemporary impressions: the change from heroic to economic politics that Sir Walter Scott had described in the Waverley novels, the planned factory community of Robert Owen's New Lanark, the visionary politics of desperate hand-loom weavers, the alarm and astonishment shown by European visitors. Only a few months later, his word was made iron in George Stephenson's *Rocket*.

But can we gain from such images a consistent set of concepts which are relevant both to us and to the age itself? G. M. Young, its pioneer explorer, in *The Portrait of an Age* (1936), saw his actors 'controlled, and animated, by the imponderable pressure of the Evangelical discipline and the almost universal faith in progress'. But Young's history—'the conversation of the people who counted'—was pretty élitist history, which neglected the mass of the people—miners and factory hands, Irish cotters, and London street arabs—or identified them solely as 'problems'. The perception, at its most acute in Tolstoy's *War and Peace*, that great movements stem from millions of individual decisions reached by ordinary people, was lacking. Few of the British contemporaries of his French and Russian soldiers shared the views of 'the people who counted': as far as we know, only a minority of them saw the inside of a church, and from what they wrote and read they had little enough faith in progress. Yet, however constrained their freedom of action, the decisions of those subjected to the 'monstrous condescension of posterity' are crucial. We have to attend to them.

E. P. Thompson, who coined this phrase, has argued that a continuing frame of interpretation did exist: the law. No matter how partial its administration—and in the eighteenth century this was often brutally apparent—'the rule of law' was still regarded as a common possession. This claim remained valid after the industrial impact. In 1832, as a young MP, Thomas Babington Macaulay argued in favour of political reform to protect the rule of law from the exercise of arbitrary power: 'Pople crushed by law have no hopes but from power. If laws are their enemies, they will be enemies to laws...' Let the law 'incorporate' new groups, and these would defer to the state system. This philosophy balanced the 'revolutionary' consequences of industrial changes, and the frequent attempts to create from these a new politics.

The evolution of law, moreover, provided a model for other social and political changes. 'The most beautiful and wonderful of the natural laws of God', in an Oxford inaugural lecture of 1859, turned out to be economics, but they might as well have been jurisprudence or geology. Personal morality, technical innovation, the very idea of Britain: the equation of law with progress bore all these together on its strong current.

Among all classes, the old morality—bribery and unbelief, drinking, wenching, and gambling—gradually became regarded as archaic if not antisocial. As well as 'vital religion', rationalist enlightenment, retailed from Scotland or France, and cheaper consumer goods indicated that life could be longer and more refined. Where Samuel Pepys had regarded his Admiralty subordinates' wives as legitimate fringe benefits, James Boswell, equally amorous, agonized about his wife and family, foreshadowing new moral imperatives—whether engendered by the evils of corruption or slavery, proletarian unrest, the French, or the wrath of the God so dramatically depicted by William Blake.

The onus of proof was on the status quo. Did it elevate? Did it improve? The English traveller, who in 1839 was appalled to find that the Hungarians had no sailing boats on their waterways when their Muslim neighbours had *dhows* on the

Danube, was typical in regarding this, whatever the reasons for it—the interests of oarsmen and horsemen, the free transport entitlement of Hungarian nobles, sheer loathing of everything Turkish—as a case of 'sinister interests' blocking reform and progress.

Neither 'progress' nor the rule of law were inevitable but had to be fought for, against internal and external enemies: 'old corruption' and new disaffection at home, powerful rivals abroad. Progress meant moral development, not economic or political manipulation—the values expressed, say, by the hero of Mrs Craik's *John Halifax, Gentleman* (1857):

Nothing that could be done did he lay aside until it was done; his business affairs were kept in perfect order, each day's work being completed with the day. And in the thousand-and-one little things that were constantly arising, from his position as magistrate and land-owner, and his general interest in the movements of the time, the same system was invariably pursued. In his relations with the world outside, as in his own little valley, he seemed determined to 'work while it was day.' If he could possibly avoid it, no application was ever unattended to; no duty left unfinished; no good unacknowledged; no evil unremedied, or at least unforgiven.

The rule of law was an English tradition, but its role as an ideology of 'efficient' government had in part been created on Britain's internal frontiers. Dragging their country out of its backwardness, the Scots had used their distinctive legal institutions as instruments for consolidating landed capital, for exploring and ordering 'civil society'. In Edinburgh, Adam Smith, William Robertson, Adam Ferguson, and David Hume wove economics, history, sociology, and philosophy together with jurisprudence to produce the complex achievement of the Scots Enlightenment. Figures such as Patrick Colquhoun, James Mill, and the 'Edinburgh Reviewers' transmitted its values south. Ireland's contribution was quite different. 'The law', Dean Swift had written, 'presumes no Catholic to breathe in Ireland.' Protestant law had, by definition, to be coercive. Not surprisingly, Ireland saw the creation of Britain's first state-organized police force, in 1814.

Although legal campaigns helped to end the serfdom of Scots colliers and salt-workers in 1799, and the British Empire's slave trade in 1807, Scots and English cottars benefited little from their role in the 'improvement' of their countryside. Law was more than ever the tool of property: a function which unified the local élites of a still-disparate society when assault from Europe threatened. The clan chiefs and lairds who had rallied to the French-backed Charles Edward in 1745 were now land-owners who had no common cause with revolutionaries. Jacobinism was as alien to them as Jacobitism. But the ensuing use of law to enforce national solidarity and safeguard economic changes was to face it with its most formidable test.

Industrial Development

A greybeard in 1815, who could remember the panic in London as the Jacobites marched through Manchester in 1745, would be struck by one important international change—the reversal in the positions of Britain and France. This was not simply the result of over twenty years of war culminating in victory at Waterloo, but of consistent industrial development and the take-over of important markets. British blockade destroyed the economy of the great French seaports: grass grew in the streets of Bordeaux, and meanwhile Britain annexed something like 20 per cent of world trade, and probably about half the trade in manufactured goods.

Industrial development did not follow a predetermined, pre-dictable route to success. The process was gradual and casual. Adam Smith regarded industry with suspicion; even in the 1820s, economists doubted whether technology could improve general living standards. Britain had certainly advanced in the century which followed Gregory King's estimate, in 1688, that mining, manufacturing, and building produced a fifth of the gross national income of England and Wales. (The *British* figure would be less, as it included backward Scotland and Ireland.) By 1800, estimates put the British 'manufacturing' figure at 25 per cent of national income and trade and transport at 23 per cent. This sort of growth, however, was not beyond French capabilities. What marked Britain off were qualitative changes, notably in patterns of marketing, technology, and government intervention—and, at 33 per cent of national product in 1800, her capitalist agriculture. While revolution retarded French farming by enhancing peasant rights, in Britain feudal title became effective ownership, the key to commercial exploitation.

In 1745 France's population, at 21 million, was double that of Britain. Her economy, thanks to royal patronage and state control, had not only a huge output but was technologically inventive and grew as rapidly as Britain's. But technology in Britain was developed by new requirements, while in France it was checked not only by government interference but by the bounty of traditional resources. France still produced ample wood for charcoal: British ironmasters had to turn to coal. France had a huge woollen industry integrated with peasant farming; in Britain, enclosure and growing agricultural efficiency set limits to such domestic industries, and encouraged the building of large industrial plants which needed water or steam power or systematized production. Above all, Britain had already won the trade war by the 1770s, pushing France out of the Spanish territories, out of India and Canada—with even the loss of her American colonies soon made good by the rise of the cotton trade.

In 1801, the first official Census found that England had 8.3 million people, Scotland 1.63 million, Wales 587,000, and Ireland 5.22 million. This settled the debate on population: it seemed to have risen by about 25 per cent since 1750, a rate of increase 50 per cent greater than the European norm. Debate still continues about why. The death-rate fell some time before 1750 (as a result of improved food supplies and better hygiene, and a diminution in the killing power of epidemics) and this was then reflected in a rising birth-rate as the greater number of surviving children entered breeding age.

In Britain, increased manufacturing activity, and the vanishing of the family farm, made children a valuable source of income. 'Away, my boys, get children,' advised the agricultural writer Arthur Young, 'they are worth more than they ever were'. In Ireland, population growth surfed along on a different wave: the desire of landlords for greater rents, and the cultivation of potatoes from the 1720s on. The latter increased the nutritive output of a patch of land by a factor of three; the former realized that a rising population on additional farms meant that each acre might yield three times its rent. The population consequently doubled in the fifty years between 1780 and 1831.

Population (*in millions*)

	1780(est.)	1801	1831	1851
England	7.1	8.30	13.1	16.92
Wales	0.43	0.59	0.91	1.06
Scotland	1.4	1.63	2.37	2.90
Ireland	4.05	5.22	7.77	6.51
Total UK	12.98	15.74	24.15	27.39
England (as %)	54.7%	52.7%	54.2%	61.8%

A recent calculation has suggested that in the early nineteenth century British agriculture was 2.5 times more productive than that of France, itself much more efficient than the rest of Europe. The result was that a population on the move from country to town, and at the same time increasing, could be fed. In 1801 about 30 per cent of the mainland British lived in towns, and 21 per cent in towns of over 10,000 population— a far higher percentage than in any north European country. Industrial towns, however, accounted for less than a quarter of this figure. Their inhabitants were outnumbered by the numbers living in seaports, dockyard towns, and regional centres. London, already a metropolis without parallel, had around 1.1 millions, over a third of the entire urban population.

Otherwise, population was still fairly evenly distributed. The counties were still increasing in absolute numbers. The 'Celtic fringe' still accounted for nearly half (45 per cent) of United Kingdom population: Dublin (165,000) and Edinburgh (83,000) still followed London in the great towns league; Cork and Limerick were larger than most manufacturing towns. The complex organization of such regional centres reflected the predominant roles of local gentry, clergy, farmers, and professional people, and the result of decades of increasing trade.

Trade more than industry still characterized the British economy. Continental towns were—or had only recently ceased to be—stringently controlled, their trade limited and taxed in complex and frustrating ways. The medieval gates of little German cities still swung shut at nightfall to keep 'foreigners' from their markets. But in Britain, by contrast, there were scarcely any impediments to internal commerce, while 'mercantilist' governments had positively encouraged the acquisition of 'treasure by foreign trade'. The eighteenth century had seen important changes. Seemingly perpetual war in the Channel and the attraction of large-scale smuggling, centred on the Isle of Man, had shifted commerce routes north. Liverpool rose on grain and slaves, then on cotton, Glasgow on tobacco and linen, then on cotton and engineering. Gradually, their entrepôt function was being changed by the opening up of efficient transport links to their hinterland, and its transformation by manufacturing industry.

Trade and distribution provided the central impulses for industrialization. No other European country had 30 per cent of its population in towns, to be fed, clothed, and warmed, or controlled such vast overseas markets. The institutions through which British merchants handled all this—which the law allowed, if not encouraged them to set up—provided a framework in which increases in productivity could be translated into profit, credit, and further investment. At home, an expanding 'respectable class' provided a market for clothes, cutlery, building materials, china; this 'domestic' demand grew by some 42 per cent between 1750 and 1800. But in the same period the increase in export industries was over 200 per cent, most of this coming in the years after 1780.

Besides agriculture, three sectors were dominant—coal, iron, and textiles. The first two provided much of the capital equipment, infrastructure, and options for future development; but textiles made up over 50 per cent of exports by value in 1750, and over 60 per cent by 1800. Cotton, insignificant in 1750, was dominant with 39 per cent in 1810. Coal output doubled between 1750 and 1800, as steam pumps enabled deeper and more productive seams to be mined, and horse-worked railways bore coal ever-greater distances to water transport. Iron production, boosted by war demand, by the use of coal instead of charcoal for smelting, and by the perfecting in the 1780s of 'puddling' and 'rolling' wrought iron, rose by 200 per cent between 1788 and 1806. But textiles were the power which towed the glider of industrialization into the air.

Wool had always been England's great speciality, though linen, dominant on the Continent, was expanding under government patronage in Ireland and Scotland. Cotton rose largely through its adaptability to machine production, and the rapid increase in the supply of raw material that slavery in the American south made possible. The new machinery was primitive. But rising demand meant that resistance to its introduction by the labour force was overcome. John Kay's fly-shuttle loom (which doubled a weaver's output), destroyed when he tried to introduce it in the 1730s, was taken up in the 1770s, along with James Hargreaves's hand-operated spinning jenny (a multiple-spindle wheel) and Richard Arkwright's water-powered spinning frame. The last, and the great factories it required, spread from the Derbyshire valleys to Lancashire and Scotland. Before competition brought prices down—by two-thirds between 1784 and 1832—huge fortunes could be made. Arkwright's shrewd exploitation of his patent rights brought him £200,000 and a baronetcy. Sir Robert Peel, calico printer and father of the future Tory premier, ended up by employing 15,000. Robert Owen reckoned that between 1799 and 1829 his New Lanark mills netted him and his partners £300,000 profit *after* paying a 5 per cent dividend. For some twenty years a modest prosperity extended, too, to the handloom weavers, before the introduction of power-looms and the flooding of the labour market with Irish immigrants and, after 1815, ex-servicemen. This turned the weavers' situation into one of the starkest tragedies of the age.

Cotton technology spread to other textiles—speedily to Yorkshire worsteds, slowly to linen and wool. But it also boosted engineering and metal construction. Powerful and reliable machinery had to be built to drive thousands of spindles; mills—tinderboxes otherwise—had to be fireproofed with metal columns and joists. In 1770, Arkwright used millwrights and clockmakers to install his mainly wooden machinery at Cromford. But mill-design and machine-building soon became a specialized job, with water-wheels of up to 150 horsepower, complex spinning mules (a powered hybrid of the jenny and the frame, spinning very fine 'counts') and the increased use of steam-power.

James Watt patented his separate-condenser steam engine in 1774, and its rotative version in 1781. By 1800, cotton mills were its chief users, as it supplied reliable and continuous power for mule spinning. In its turn, the increasingly sophisticated technology required by the steam engine enhanced both its further application—to locomotives in 1804, to shipping in 1812—and the development of the machine-tool industry, particularly associated with Henry Maudslay and his invention of the screw-cutting lathe. This (and its associated invention, the micrometer) made possible the absolutely accurate machining of parts. From now on, machines could reproduce themselves and be constructed in ever-greater complexity. The standards of the eighteenth-century clockmaker were no longer an expensive skill, but part of the conventional wisdom of mechanical engineering.

The creation of a transport infrastructure made for a golden age of civil engineering, too, as men such as Brindley, Smeaton, Telford, and Rennie strove to exploit water-carriage and horse-power as efficiently as possible. In a parallel exploitation of wind-power, sailing ships became so sophisticated that they remained competitive with steam until the 1880s. The country's awful roads were repaired and regulated, and in some cases built from scratch, by turnpike trusts, even by government. It took nearly a fortnight to travel from London to Edinburgh in 1745, two and a half days in 1796, and around 36 hours by coach or steamer in 1830. Building on the steady growth of river navigation in the seventeenth century, 'dead-water' canals using pound locks were being built in Ireland in the 1730s. But it was the duke of Bridgewater's schemes to link Manchester with a local coalfield and Liverpool, 1760–71, that showed the importance of water transport for industrial growth. Bridgewater's engineer, Brindley, devised 'narrow' canals to prevent water loss in the 'dry' Midlands, and during the peace of 1764–72, when money was cheap, companies of gentry, merchants, manufacturers, and bankers managed to link all the major navigable rivers. Such private enterprise could pay, in the case of the Oxford canal, up to 30 per cent in dividend, but the average was about 8 per cent. The next boom, in the 1780s, pushed the system beyond what was commercially feasible, but Britain now had a transport network without parallel in Europe, while the unity of 'improvers', agricultural and industrial, in this cause overcame many of the barriers to further co-operation.

Reform and Religion

The British government did not play, or wish to play, a positive role in industrialization; as the Corn Laws of 1815 were to show, neither did it abstain in the interests of *laissez-faire*. But increasingly it observed principles which were more or less systematic, and less unfavourable to industrial capitalists than they were to any other class—except, of course, landowners, who were frequently capitalists themselves in mining, transport, and property development. The axioms of Blackstone and Burke: of continuity, the division of powers, the interpenetration of government, economy, and society—and above all the notion of government as a self-regulating mechanism—complemented the mechanics of classical economics, the discoveries of science, and even the cultivated deism of the upper classes.

But the ideal required renovation. Corruption and inefficiency had taken their toll at the time of the American War, and although the spectacle of mob violence—particularly in the Gordon Riots of 1780—made respectable reformers more circumspect, reform was an admitted necessity. The messages of Adam Smith and John Wesley had, in their various ways, seen to that. The problem was, how could it be kept within constitutional bounds? Attempts such as the Association movement to make politics more principled and symmetrical simply exposed the ramifications of 'interest' and downright corruption. The 'vast rotten borough' of Scotland, where only 4,000-odd electors returned 45 placemen MPs (only one man in 114 had the vote, compared with one in seven in England), got its reward in the patronage distributed by its 'managers' the Dundas family, notably in the East India Company and the Admiralty. Ireland's 'free' Parliament, after 1782, was still an institution for which no Catholic could vote.

The opinion of the great manufacturing towns had to be articulated by pressure groups such as the General Chamber of Manufacturers, because of the gross maldistribution of political power. In 1801 the 700,000 people of Yorkshire had only two county and 26 borough MPs, while the 188,000 people of Cornwall had two county and 42 borough MPs. Dissenters and Catholics were allowed to vote after 1793 but could not sit in Parliament. On the other hand, so restricted was the impact of politics, and so expensive the business of getting on in it, that for some exclusion was a positive benefit. Although their overall numbers were in decline, the elaborate family relationships of the Quakers (who could not 'marry out' and remain in the sect) underpinned widely scattered enterprises ranging from iron and lead-smelting works to banks and railways. The liberal-minded Unitarians, who 'believed in one God at most',

THE CANAL SYSTEM IN THE EARLY NINETEENTH CENTURY

were energetic leaders of provincial enlightenment in science and education.

Somewhat different was the Evangelical revival. Populist and traditional high church in origin, this drew inspiration from the religious heritage of the seventeenth century—exemplified by Bunyan, and broadcast by John Wesley—and from the devotional literature of such as William Law. In contrast to 'Old Dissent' and Calvinist 'election', it stressed that grace was available to those who directed their life by biblical precept. It was respectable without being exclusive, ecumenical and diffusely 'enthusiastic' (many who were to become its severest agnostic and high-church critics started as devout Evangelicals)—a faith of crisis, valid against atheistic revolution, unfeeling industrial relationships, and brutal personal behaviour. Pitt drank and Fox gambled, but both were susceptible to the sort of pressure which well-placed Evangelicals could exert.

The Evangelical revival was politically conservative, yet it soon flowed into peculiar channels. In 1795 the 'Society of Methodists' founded by Wesley left the Church of England because they could no longer accept conventional ordination. Tories they remained, but further Methodist groups such as the Primitives (who seceded in 1811) became more autonomous and more radical. Methodism was northern—'the real religion of Yorkshire'—elsewhere the Baptists and Congregationalists expanded in industrial towns whose élites were frequently Unitarian or Quaker. George Eliot described dissenting values in her 'political novel' about 1832, *Felix Holt* (1867):

Here was a population not convinced that Old England was as good as possible; here were multitudinous men and women aware that their religion was not exactly the religion of their rulers, who might therefore be better than they were, and who, if better, might alter many things which now made the world perhaps more painful than it need be, and certainly more sinful.

'Vital religion' accomplished a religious revolution in Wales. In 1800 over 80 per cent of the population still adhered to the established Church whose mid-eighteenth-century missionary efforts, the 'circulating schools', had increased literacy (in Welsh) and enthusiasm beyond the point where it could sustain it. Into the vacuum flowed Calvinistic Methodism and the other nonconformist bodies; by 1851, Wales was 80 per cent chapel-going. In Scotland, the established Presbyterian Church, which controlled education and poor relief, was practically a subordinate legislature. Controlled by the landowners and their worldly, liberal clergy, it was coming under increasing assault not only from independent Presbyterians, but from those, usually Evangelicals, who wished to transfer power to the congregations. In Ireland, the dissenting tradition was initially liberal, its leaders comparing their legal disadvantages with those of the Catholics. But the events of the 1790s, and the recrudescence of Evangelical fundamentalism was ultimately to intensify the divide between the Protestant north-east and the rest of the country.

The Wars Abroad

The French Revolution was greeted with general enthusiasm in Britain. At worst, it would weaken the old enemy; at best it would create another constitutional state. Charles James Fox, James Watt, Joseph Priestley, the young Wordsworth, and Coleridge all celebrated it; Robert Burns was inspired to write 'Scots wha' hae'—which had obvious contemporary implications. Even the government was slow to echo Edmund Burke's severe censure in his *Reflections on the Revolution in France*, published in November 1790, while it still seemed a modest constitutional movement. Although Burke expressed what the establishment felt, especially when Paris lurched leftwards in June 1791: remove customary deference and force would rule. Reform should be permitted only on terms which retained the basic political structure. Burke both attacked France and dramatized Blackstone's defence of the British political system. The establishment became really alarmed by the

Anglo-American radical Tom Paine's reply, *The Rights of Man* (1791–2), with its bold proposals for individualist, democratic reform. Burke may himself have started what he tried to avoid. If the *Reflections* sold 19,000 copies in six months, *The Rights of Man* sold 200,000—an incredible total for a society still only semi-literate. Pamphleteering had not demonstrated this range and impact since the Civil War.

The government was alarmed by two things above all—the impact of French notions of 'self-determination' on Britain's Low Country client states, and the contagion of ideas. The European monarchies, with even greater grounds for concern, abandoned the gentlemanly rules of eighteenth-century war in summer 1792 and treated the French as rabid dogs to be shot. The French reciprocated with the notion of war as a popular crusade: 'a nation in arms'. In Britain, the diplomatic threat worked on the political threat: warnings to France increased the conviction of some optimistic revolutionaries in Paris that war would lead to a British revolution. On 1 February 1793 France declared war.

Britain was unprepared. The army had only 45,000 men; scarcely a tenth of the battle-fleet could put to sea. Moreover, the war was quite different from earlier Anglo-French conflicts. The new style of army, the intensity of the revolutionary attack, the competence of France's new commanders: together these put Britain's allies in trouble from the start. By 1797 Austria had been knocked out and Britain stood alone against Bonaparte's Armée d'Angleterre.

Three things preoccupied the government in those early war years: the threat of invasion, the cost of the war, and the problem of combating internal dissension. The French made three invasion attempts, once via Wales and twice via Ireland. A landing in Pembrokeshire in 1797 found no support, but in autumn 1798 a force commanded by General Humbert landed at Killala in Mayo and, with local allies, campaigned for two weeks until defeated. The government hoped to defend the mainland by fortifying the coast with Martello towers, embodying the Militia (the home defence force), and extending the Militia Acts to Scotland and Ireland. All this gave ceaseless headaches to the part-time local officials involved. As subsidies to allies were running into tens of millions by 1795, taxation had to be radically increased and included, after 1799, the innovation of an income tax levied at 2s. (10p) in the pound. Finally the government acted drastically against groups which sought peace or solidarity with the French. 'Pitt's reign of terror' in 1793–4, supplemented by the local activities of magistrates, industrialists, and patriotic societies, destroyed many of the radical societies. The repression was particularly fierce in Scotland, where Lord Braxfield's brutal Doric humour arbitrarily upheld 'the most perfect constitution ever created'.

Braxfield's sarcasms—on being told by one of his victims that Jesus was a reformer, his reply was 'Muckle he made o' that. He waur hangit tae!'—symbolized the end of the upper-class liberalism of the Scottish enlightenment. Thirty years of fairly constant repression followed, wielded by Pitt's Scottish lawyer allies, the Dundas family.

In Ireland, the reversal was even more drastic. War led Pitt to pressurize the Irish Parliament into granting Catholics voting rights in 1793, in an attempt to win them from enthusiasm for 'godless' France. But the non-sectarian radicalism of the United Irishmen rapidly grew. By 1798, it was countered in Ulster by the ultra-Protestant Orange Lodges and by the local violence of a Catholic peasantry bitterly resentful at Protestant privileges, and in part influenced by French-trained priests imbued with revolutionary ideals. Shortly before Humbert landed there was a vicious, though short-lived, outburst in Wicklow, enough to convince the Protestant ascendancy of its isolation. In 1800 Ireland followed the example of the Scots in 1707, and entered into political union with England.

Apart from the brief interlude of 1801–3, the 'wars abroad' lasted until 1815. By then, Britain had spent £1,500 million on war; yet the effects were ambiguous and curiously limited. The war was soon erased from popular memory. Britain was an armed camp for much of the time: there were constant drafts into the militia, and at any stage about a sixth of the adult male population may have been under arms. Compared with France, few of these actually served abroad, although many—around 210,000—died. What was in France a demographic set-back— her population increased by 32 per cent, 1800–50, compared with Britain's 50 per cent—had a different, smaller impact on Britain. Yet British naval supremacy was never challenged after 1805, and through blockade it destroyed much of French industry, whose most dynamic sectors were based on the trading ports.

Adam Smith had written that war would distort demand and create a 'seller's market' among certain types of labour. It proceeded to do so. The iron trade boomed not only in its traditional base of the West Midlands, but in central Scotland and also in South Wales, where Merthyr Tydfil expanded twenty-fold in population between 1790 and 1820—a raw, remote city (accessible, incredibly, by canal) in a country whose largest mid-eighteenth-century town, Carmarthen, had contained scarcely 4,000 people. As blockade throttled her rivals, Britain's ever more commanding lead in textiles reached the stage where her manufacturers were clothing French armies. The huge naval dockyards of Chatham, Portsmouth, and Devonport were further expanded and became pioneers of mass production. Their creations, the sailing warships, were dramatically improved; steam-power, when it took over in the 1850s, was almost a lesser revolution.

The navy, in fact, typified many of government's problems. The wretched condition of the sailors provoked mutinies at Spithead and the Nore in 1797. These had little political content; the mutineers, however aggrieved, remained overwhelmingly patriotic. They were dealt with by a mixture of coercion and concession—as indeed were the well-organized dockyard workers. Elsewhere, government reacted ambiguously to attempts to remedy working-class distress. The Combination Laws of 1799 treated trade unions like revolutionary societies and outlawed them; government also successfully opposed attempts to secure legal minimum wages and restore older industrial relationships, even when these were backed by manufacturers (on the whole smaller ones). Such measures, and the depressions which resulted from the diversion of investment into government funds and the trade war, ensured that average real wages stagnated between 1790 and 1814. Yet the relatively generous poor relief scales adopted by many rural parishes after the 1790s—the so-called Speenhamland system—continued a traditional entitlement to relief, and undoubtedly mitigated even sharper social conflicts.

For most of the war Britain avoided European involvement, and paid subsidies instead to the members of the various coalitions she assembled, first against revolutionary France, then against Napoleon. This was simply a refinement of the mercenary principles of eighteenth-century wars. Only between 1811 and 1814, when she sent her own troops to the Peninsula, did her army take on a European role. The gains in other areas, however, were immense; her hold over India was strengthened, and she achieved effective dominance, through Singapore, of the Dutch East Indies; she conquered Ceylon between 1795 and 1816, took over South Africa from the Dutch, and established a claim on Egypt. Informally, she secured a trading hegemony over the former Spanish colonies of Central and South America.

Although Britain was victorious, the war's imprint on Europe was predominantly French. Wherever Napoleon's armies went, they left (or their opponents copied) the laws, the measurements, the administration—and above all the nationalistic ethos—of the revolution. The map had been totally changed. Before 1789, Britain had been part of a continental community. David Hume and Adam Smith were as much at home in Paris as they were in Edinburgh, and rather more, perhaps, than they were in London. After 1815, Britain, despite the economic progress which attracted hundreds of foreign visitors, remained at a distance from European life.

At home, war and depression polarized political ideas into 'revolutionary' and 'loyalist'. 'Pitt's reign of terror', patriotic societies, and church-and-king mobs pushed democratic thinkers, earlier commonplace enough, either into obscurity or into alliance with genuinely oppressed groups like the Irish or the working class. The 'Jacobin tradition' became as sensitive to industrial and economic change as it had been to the 'evils' of established government. A diffuse, volatile blend of everything from anarchism to religious millenarianism, it continued to mark working-class movements up to and including Chartism.

Paradoxically, however, the relentlessly practical approach of the governing élite, and the role of repression in exalting state power over contractual ideas of politics, conjured up its own radical rival. Evangelicalism, in the hands of William Wilberforce and the Clapham Sect, aimed at converting the élite; but so too did the reiterated schemes of Jeremy Bentham, a wealthy lawyer who believed, more or less, that society could be governed through a set of self-evident principles analogous to those of economics. Of these, the most easily grasped was 'utilitarianism'—that social action should aim at producing 'the greatest good for the greatest number'. The sworn foe to all ideals of 'social contract', Bentham opposed the French Revolution, and tried to interest successive British governments in his schemes, particularly of law and prison reform. He was probably more successful than he thought, but frustrations drove him towards the democratic reformers and by 1815 he was supporting universal suffrage. The 'philosophic radicals', as Bentham's disciples were called, offered the combination of institutional reform with political continuity—and, after 1815, offered it to both sides, as they built up a following of moderate working-class leaders. From this stemmed both a centralized pattern of state action, and a theory of public intervention, which remained powerfully influential for the rest of the century.

Benthamite theory saw local authorities raising rates and taking executive action in appropriately-sized districts. They would be supervised by salaried inspectors reporting to a central board. 'Old corruption' and popular profligacy would thus be supposedly checked; local responsibility would be retained. But, in fact, the officials were dominant. Bentham and his acolytes, the Mills, father and son, and Edwin Chadwick, may have been converted to democracy, but they were reluctant to let the people's representatives do more than veto the officials' actions. Not surprisingly, their most spectacular successes were gained in British India.

Law had shifted into a class pattern. Working men, accustomed to fight disabilities in the courts, lost traditional rights and had their independent action constrained. The alarm of the propertied classes gave teeth to hitherto ineffective sanctions. The 'making of the English working class' was, at least in part, a reaction to a combination of war, industrialization, and repression: it meant a hostility to inequitable law. There was little respect for 'the Thing' (the undeclared confederacy of the rich to exhaust the poor) in William Cobbett; practical ignorance of it, in Robert Owen. Even the Benthamites thought the legal establishment a 'vast sinister interest'. Although ultimately only the Irish stood out against it, the triumph of the rule of law, like Waterloo, proved 'a damned close-run thing'. It was probably only possible because popular expectations of it endured long enough to be sustained by a new wave of constitutional agitation.

Roads to Freedom

> Men of England, wherefore plough
> For the Lords who lay ye low?
> Wherefore weave with toil and care
> The rich robes your tyrants wear?
>
> .   .   .   .   .
>
> Shrink to your cellars, holes and cells;
> In halls ye deck another dwells.
> Why shake the chains ye wrought? Ye see
> The steel ye tempered glance on ye.
>
> Shelley, *To the Men of England*

The post-war Tory government after 1815 encountered a new set of literary radicals. Coleridge and Wordsworth, gathered to the bosom of the forces of order, were succeeded by Byron and Shelley. Lord Liverpool's administration of 1812–27 was in fact a pretty bourgeois affair, made up of minor gentry, the sons of doctors and merchants, and even (in the case of George Canning) an actress. Although condemned as reactionary—which some of its members certainly were—it sat edgily on the right centre. It was liberal (by the standards of Restoration Europe) abroad, and conciliatory at home. But it inherited a fearsome post-war slump and racking industrial tensions, on top of a war debt to be paid for, and demobilized servicemen to be settled. It was scarcely aided by an able Whig opposition, which lacerated it through the medium of the new literary reviews, and a rich culture of popular protest, from the 'unstamped' newspapers of Henry Hetherington and Richard Carlile to the bucolic radicalism of William Cobbett and the visionary millenarianism of William Blake. The landed interest pressed for, and obtained, the maintenance of subsidy on grain through the Corn Law of 1815; this probably staved off, for over a decade, discontent among those of the working population who tilled the land. But it was all at a cost. Even more than in 1811–12, the threat to order came from the new industrial towns, where the end of the post-war boom caused widespread unemployment and a steep fall in wages. The consciousness of the workers, more of their *industrial* than of their class position, had steadily sharpened since 1800, and the local representatives of government, industrialists and Justices of the Peace, felt their isolation acutely.

Do the fears that these gentry frequently expressed—of Jacobin mobs baying at their gates—and the explicitly revolutionary ideas of some leaders of the working classes, add up to a real threat to overthrow the regime, which was only narrowly averted? They might have done, had action been co-ordinated, had a common economic cause existed to bind industrial workers to the parliamentary radicals and the skilled trades of the capital, and had the governing classes really lost their nerve.

But this would have been very difficult to achieve. London was not an 'absolute' capital like Paris; there were few vital levers of power to be grasped—had the London radicals mobilized *en masse*.

London did not move with the provinces. The parliamentary opposition disowned and deprecated violence, and the Home Office under its repressive head, Viscount Sidmouth, and his local agents cowed resistance—but at a price. The climax came in Manchester on 16 August 1819, when the local magistracy ordered the yeomanry to apprehend speakers at a huge but peaceful reform demonstration in St. Peter's Fields. The soldiers turned on the crowd and eleven were killed at 'Peterloo'. Both the desire of radicals for revenge and the penetration of the radical movement by government spies and *agents provocateurs* were responsible for further outbreaks in the following year—a weavers' rising in Scotland and the 'Cato Street conspiracy' to assassinate the Cabinet in London. Repression—the gallows and transportation—was sharp, savage, and effective, but in the long term it strengthened constitutional resistance and steadily discredited the government.

The government itself looked askance at unbound industrialization. Moving towards free trade, systematic administration, and a reformed penal code, it still depended on the agricultural interest, and feared further working-class violence. Sir Walter Scott, its supporter, regretted the shift of industry to the towns, since he believed that in country mills the manufacturer 'exercised a salutary influence over men depending on and intimately connected with him and his prospects'. He probably had Robert Owen and New Lanark in mind. Propagandizing for self-governing industrial communities, Owen wanted to put a brake on industry and, through spade-cultivation, make agriculture again a great employer. His 'new moral world' fitted into the atmosphere of social peril and Utopian salvation which had been pervasive since the end of the war.

> The Strongest Poison ever known
> Came from Caesar's Laurel Crown.

> Nought can deform the Human Race
> Like to the Armour's iron brace.
> When Gold & Gems adorn the Plow
> To peaceful Arts shall Envy bow.

Artisans did not need to understand the artisan genius William Blake's cosmology to appreciate the message. The future must have seemed to many as apocalyptic as the huge but enormously detailed and didactic paintings of John Martin, which had a great vogue as engravings in the mid-1820s.

The Whig contribution to the political battle was, however, effective enough. In 1820 George IV's attempt to divorce his consort led to the royal family's dirty linen being washed in the courts. Henry Brougham, a leading contributor to the *Edinburgh Review*, championed Queen Caroline (not the most promising of martyrs) against king and ministry, to the plaudits of the public. Then in August 1822 Castlereagh, who as Foreign Secretary had managed to extricate Britain from the conservative powers represented in Metternich's Congresses, killed himself. The way was open for the more liberal side of the Liverpool government to show itself.

Castlereagh's successor at the Foreign Office, George Canning, sided with the American president Monroe in 1823 in guaranteeing the new republics of South America—and incidentally confirmed Britain's privileged access to a vast new market. Two years later the ministry repealed the Six Acts and anti-trade union legislation, and in 1826 it ended the 'management' of Scotland by the Dundases. The duke of Wellington's administration passed Catholic Emancipation in 1829. It bowed to Daniel O'Connell's expert management of Irish public opinion, and to the threat of a national uprising when O'Connell was elected as MP for County Clare in 1828 but, as a Catholic, was debarred from taking his seat.

Only parliamentary reform remained to be implemented, but here a direct party issue was involved. Pressure groups—the trade unions, the Scots, the Irish—could be bought off with judicious concessions. Reform, however, would mean a triumph for the Whigs, with all that meant in terms of parliamentary command and patronage. In 1828 the duke had dug his heels in, under pressure from his 'Ultras', but in the following year they parted from him over Catholic Emancipation. Meanwhile in the country agitation grew, and the Whigs did not scruple to encourage their radical rivals. Pressure rose to a peak after the Whigs under Earl Grey and Lord John Russell won the election which the death of George IV occasioned in 1830. When their Reform Bill was rejected by the Lords, well-organized 'Political Unions' held monster rallies in the cities; rioters attacked Nottingham Castle and the bishop's palace in Bristol, both seats of anti-Reform peers; in Merthyr riots were followed by the execution of a workers' leader, Dic Penderyn. In April 1832 the Lords gave way—by nine votes—much to the relief of Grey's government, which had shown its otherwise conservative nature by the brutal suppression of farm labourers' discontent—the 'Captain Swing' riots—in southern England.

Coping with Reform

Despite the near-revolutionary nature of the reform agitation, the act of 1832 incorporated the most potentially troublesome sectors of industrial and commercial power, but did little more. Scotland's electorate shot up from 4,579 to 64,447 (a 1,407 per cent increase), but that of Ireland increased by only 21 per cent; 41 large English towns—including Manchester, Bradford, and Birmingham—got representation for the first time, but the average size of an English borough electorate—and these returned almost half (324) of the total of 658 MPs—remained under 900. The 349 electors of Buckingham still returned as many MPs as the 4,172 electors of Leeds. England, with 54 per cent of the population, continued to return 71 per cent of the Commons. Before 1832 it had returned 74 per cent. 'Virtual representation', of interests rather than people, remained a principle, and

Parliament continued to be dominated by the landed interest for almost a further half-century.

Some conservatives now feared a Benthamite assault on the aristocracy and the Church. But there were few doctrinaires in Parliament, and the reforming zeal of the Whigs rapidly waned. Humanitarians got their way in 1833 with the abolition of slavery in the British Empire and the regulation of children's work in textile factories by the Factory Inspectorate. The Poor Law Amendment Act of 1834, which its architect Edwin Chadwick saw as the basis of a systematic and economical reconstruction of English local government, remained, however, an isolated monument—as much hated by the people as were its symbols, the gaunt Union Workhouses or 'bastilles'.

The Times, too, was loud in abuse of the New Poor Law, feeling perhaps that philosophical radicalism had gone far enough. For 1834 was a traumatic year. Ireland was quiet for once, the Whigs edging towards an understanding with O'Connell, which lasted for the rest of the decade, but on the mainland the 'alternative society' of the still-inchoate working class reached its apogee. The growth of trade unions, led by men such as John Doherty; the arguments of the 'unstamped' press; the frustration of radicals with the Reform Act; the return to politics of Robert Owen—all combined to produce a project for a Grand National Consolidated Trades Union which would destroy the capitalist system through a 'grand national holiday' or general strike. After this, society would be re-organized on a co-operative basis, with money values calculated in terms of hours of labour performed. Government counter-attacked in March with the victimization of six Dorset labourers—the 'Tolpuddle Martyrs'; the GNCTU undertook too many protests and strikes, which its organizers could not co-ordinate. Owen pulled out in August and effectively brought the movement to an end. On 16 October Parliament accidentally burned down; six months earlier this might have appeared more than simply symbolic.

The Whig triumph really came with local government reform. Scottish burgh councils, hitherto self-elected, were put under a rate-payer franchise in 1833; reform of the English towns followed two years later. In the larger towns, Whigs and radicals came into the fruits of office, and by and large stayed there. But the government was now badly split. In November 1834 the Tories, now under Peel and more or less pledged to work within the framework of reform, took office. A false dawn, this: the Whigs were back in April 1835, but under the deeply conservative Melbourne. When they fell from power in 1841 Peel seemed more acutely to reflect the spirit of gradualist reform, an outlook shared with 'the young queen's serious-minded consort, Albert of Saxe-Coburg-Gotha.

Peel, however, was threatened from two sides. Manufacturers, concerned at falling profits, demanded lower wages, and believed that they could only get them if the price of bread was reduced (bread was the staple diet of the working class—they ate about five pounds of it per head per week). This could only be done by permitting the free import of grain, in other words by repealing the Corn Law of 1815. Radicals, frustrated by Whig backsliding, climbed on to the band-waggon and grabbed the reins. Richard Cobden, a none-too-successful cotton merchant with transatlantic interests, John Bright, a Quaker carpet manufacturer from Rochdale, and James Wilson, the Scottish journalist who founded the *Economist* in 1843, became leading figures in the Anti-Corn Law League, inaugurated at a meeting in Manchester in October 1838. The League both represented, and in part created, the commercial-minded individualistic middle class—what the Germans called (and still call) 'Manchestertum'. By petitions, demonstrations, the mobilization of nonconformity, the imaginative use of the new penny post (1841), it created a widespread animus against the territorial aristocracy, and against Peel himself.

Peel had, in fact, followed most of the precepts of political economy in his public finance: duties on imports were drastically reduced, the Bank of England reorganized, railway promotion allowed to have its free enterprise head (despite the predilection of William Gladstone, the President of the Board of Trade, for outright nationalization). But the Leaguers acted with the fury of the desperate. They realized that their prosperity was borne on the back of an increasingly mutinous labour force. An extremely unorthodox Manchester cotton-master, the young German Friedrich Engels, watched the successive waves of discontent breaking against the mill-walls, and prophesied:

The moment the workers resolve to be bought and sold no longer, when, in the determination of the value of labour, they take the part of men possessed of a will as well as of working power, at that moment the whole Political Economy of today is at an end.

Engels's chosen instruments were the ultimate in economic depressions, and the power of the organized working class expressed in Chartism.

'I cares nothing about politics neither; but I'm a chartist' a London scavenger told Henry Mayhew, the pioneer social investigator, in 1848. The People's Charter, with its celebrated six points—manhood suffrage, the ballot, equal electoral districts, abolition of property qualifications for MPs, payment for MPs, and annual Parliaments—achieved the same immediate impact as the French Revolution and Daniel O'Connell's campaigns in Ireland. But this only gave a superficial and episodic unity to an immensely complex, highly localized movement. Formally it was ultra-democratic (although only as far as men were concerned—a proposal for female suffrage was an early casualty). In its most dramatic nation-wide phase it was also short-lived, lasting from 1838 to 1842. But organization, and heterodoxy, bubbled away in the regions, influenced by the local economic predicaments, political traditions, and the character of the leaders. The division between 'physical-' and 'moral-force' leaders was complicated by attitudes to the established parties, to the drink question, Ireland, property, and education. In Scotland and the English Midlands, leadership came from small tradesmen with a sprinkling of business and professional men. In Yorkshire it was militant, following heavy unemployment and the impact of the New Poor Law, but participated with the Tories in their campaign for factory reform. The 'frontier towns' of industrial Wales had already seen plenty of 'collective bargaining by riot', so it was possibly not surprising that a huge protest demonstration at Newport, on 4 November 1839, ended as a bloody confrontation with the military. Fourteen were killed, but subsequent trials led to transportation to Tasmania, not the gallows.

Peel was more humane and tactful than Melbourne in 1831 or Liverpool in 1819, and his policy succeeded. The economic boom of 1843 and 1844 sapped Chartism; its last revival in 1848 reflected the agony of Ireland rather than the ambitions of the English artisans, or any desire to emulate events in Europe. Late Chartism was more experimental and variegated, as well as more Irish. Feargus O'Connor projected land settlement schemes, Owenite and socialist ideas came back, along with ideas culled from European revolutionaries, many of whom ended up as exiles in Britain. But however fascinating intellectually the friendship of Julian Harney and Ernest Jones with Marx and Engels, the mass movement was dead. Old Chartists remained active in single-issue movements such as temperance, co-operation (the Rochdale Pioneer store of 1844 had Chartist origins), or trade unionism. Others emigrated. Many former Chartists ended up quite respectably integrated into mid-Victorian local government and the new provincial press.

'Unless the Lord build the City . . .'

In 1832 an appalling cholera epidemic, sweeping through Europe from the Middle East, probably killed 31,000 in Britain; in 1833 Parliament voted a £30,000 grant to elementary education, and John Keble preached at Oxford on 'national apostasy'. These events merely coincided with political reform—Parliament spent more time and money on the stables of Windsor Castle than on the education grant—but were important determinants of the direction that subsequent state action took, and the way in which the early Victorians rationalized their social position.

Cholera dramatized the problem of rapid urban growth, though its impact could be as deadly in the countryside. The new industrial towns were small in area, and densely packed, as walking to work was universal. Urban land usage accorded with economic power: the numerically tiny property-owning class, possibly less than 5 per cent of the population in a cotton town, often occupied 50 per cent of the land area. Working people lived where factories, roads, canals, and, later, railways allowed them to. The results were squalid—nineteenth-century towns smoked and stank—and, for the workers, expensive both in terms of rent and of human life. A tolerable house might take a quarter of a skilled man's weekly income, and few families were ever in a position to afford this. As a result, not only did slums multiply in the old inner-city area—the rookeries of London, the cellar-dwellings of Liverpool and Manchester, the 'lands' of the Scottish burghs, 'China' in Merthyr Tydfil—but new regionally-specific types of slum were created by landlords and speculative builders—the 'back-to-backs' of Yorkshire and the tiny 'room and kitchen' or 'single-end' flats in which 70 per cent of Glasgow families lived by 1870.

If housing was bad, sanitation was worse. Better-off citizens could combine to create commissions to provide water and sewerage, light the streets, and provide some sort of policing, but if anything, this worsened the plight of their poorer neighbours. A middle-class area's new water-closets all too often drained into the working class's water supply.

Epidemics were the working class's revenge. Surrounded by masses of the very poor in the shape of servants and tradespeople (whom they usually ignored) the wealthy suddenly became intensely vulnerable. A. C. Tait, a future Archbishop of Canterbury, for example, lost five of his seven children to scarlet fever in Carlisle in 1856. In 1831 the government forced local notables to serve on temporary boards of health, in order to combat cholera. In 1840 Edwin Chadwick, concerned at the numbers driven into pauperism by the death of the breadwinner and ill-health, conducted on behalf of the Poor Law Commissioners an *Inquiry into the Sanatory Condition of the*

Labouring Population, published in 1842. As a result of this, and subsequent agitation, not to speak of the threat of another cholera outbreak, an act of 1848 gave municipalities powers to set up local boards of health, subject to three Public Health Commissioners, among them Chadwick himself. Besides the Benthamites, other forces had been mobilized—some Chartists and radicals, but probably more Tories, professional men, and philanthropists. Exemplifying the movement as a whole was Lord Ashley. The future earl of Shaftesbury could be a prejudiced low-church Tory—Macaulay referred to his style as 'the bray of Exeter Hall'—but he inherited Wilberforce's skills at manipulating public, and élite, opinion to secure effective government intervention. In the 1840s and 1850s these skills were used to help miners, factory hands, poor emigrants, and slum-dwellers. Some have argued that administrative reform took on a dynamic of its own, independent both of parliamentary action and ideology. 'The Tory interpretation of history' (as this view has somewhat unfairly been called) contrasted the power of officials—'the men on the spot'—and enthusiasts like Ashley virtually to create their own laws, with Parliament's indifference to social conditions. But this is only a partial explanation of the reform process. Standards of conduct among officials varied from department to department, and between individuals. Some were dedicated to the point of self-sacrifice, others reflected the easy-going ethos of a civil service still recruited by patronage. Anthony Trollope, as a senior official of the Post Office, still found time to hunt twice a week, and turn out a steady 1.7 novels per annum—one of which, *The Three Clerks* (1857), gives an engaging picture of a backwater of the unreformed civil service, and Trollope's own sour observations on its reformers.

As this was the golden age both of 'local self-government' and of professional evolution, the strongest initiatives came from the great cities, and from a new generation of largely Scottish-trained doctors, who were making the transition from lowly surgeon-apothecaries into a self-governing profession. Liverpool appointed the first Medical Officer of Health in 1847;

the City of London, a 'square mile' rich in every variety of social peril, appointed the dynamic Dr John Simon a year later. By 1854 the appointment of Medical Officers of Health was compulsory, and proved critical not only in getting the cities to undertake major water, drainage, and slum clearance schemes, but to ensure that regulations on building and overcrowding were enforced.

The new industrial society brought into question the organization of education. Opinions on this differed: the Evangelical Hannah More believed that to inculcate religion but preserve order, children should learn to read but not write. Adam Smith, fearing the intellectually stultifying impact of the division of labour on the working class, sought to mitigate it by state education. Although this existed in Scotland, as a result of the Calvinist reformation of the Kirk, there was no English equivalent. Before the 1800s, there were grammar schools, frequently of pre-reformation origin, independent or 'adventure' schools, and charity schools. These varied enormously in quality, and could never accommodate an expanding and youthful population, let alone service the new urban areas and improve standards. Around 1800, however, opinion—including even that of George III—swung towards education as a prophylactic against revolution—partly through the appearance of new, cheap, and thus seductive forms of teaching. The 'monitorial' systems of Lancaster and Bell, whereby senior pupils learned lessons by rote and then instructed their juniors, led directly to the foundation of the British and Foreign Schools Society in 1808, and the National Society in 1811. These two attempts at national coverage, however, coincided with the exacerbation of hostilities between their respective sponsors, the nonconformists and the established Church; religious animus continued to take precedence over educational criteria for nearly a century.

Religious antagonisms in the reform of the endowed, or 'public', schools were internal to Anglicanism, and less fierce. The schools' condition, peculiarly wretched in the last years of the eighteenth century, had improved even before the radical

Broad-Churchman Thomas Arnold began his career at Rugby in 1829. His reforms, in fact, paralleled the essentially conservative political settlement of 1832, but lasted far longer. A 'liberal education' (Latin and Greek) remained dominant among those destined for the universities, but it was elevated from a totally meaningless ritual for young aristocrats into the subject-matter of competitive advancement, through scholarships and, at Oxford and Cambridge, college fellowships, for middle-class boys. Their goals were the prizes of subsidized entry into the professions, but their function was more profound: to act as bell-wethers guiding other boys from the commercial middle class into a sanitized version of the values of the territorial aristocracy. By the time he died in 1842, Arnold was being imitated at the other older public schools, and the movement proceeded, aided by the expansion of the railway system and, in 1857, by Thomas Hughes's remarkably successful *Tom Brown's Schooldays*.

The remodelling of the public schools provided a paradigm for a new generation of reformers, many of whom had been educated there. Unlike the Benthamites, they developed no highly-integrated programme, but rather sought to convert institutions accessible only to the aristocracy and the Anglican clergy to serve the whole of society. This ideal of 'nationalization' with its corollary, the 'incorporation' of the working class into 'political society', was expressed in 1848 by the Christian Socialist followers of F. D. Maurice—including Tom Hughes—in their attempt to make the Church of England an arbiter between capital and labour. They were not alone. In Bradford William Edward Forster, a young radical woollen manufacturer, formerly a Quaker, wrote:

Unless some concessions be made to these masses, and unless all classes strive earnestly to keep them better fed, first or last there will be a convulsion; but I believe the best political method of preventing it is by the middle class sympathising with the operatives, and giving themselves power to oppose their unjust claims by helping them in those which are reasonable.

Forster's wife was the daughter of Arnold of Rugby, the sister of Matthew Arnold, inspector of schools and poet. The 'intellectual aristocracy' of high thinking and moderate reform was already shifting from evangelical religion to political intervention.

Arnold, the public schools, and most of the politicians belonged to the Broad Church or liberal Anglican tradition, whose principles envisaged the Church as partner of the State, a relationship to which theological doctrine was strictly subordinate. The Evangelicals exalted religious sanctions, but their simple theology was being corroded by liberal assaults, which seemed to reach a climax with the Reform Act of 1832. Clergymen feared that a tide of Benthamite, and hence atheistic, reform would be unleashed; John Keble in an Oxford sermon declared a clerical resistance which would be founded on the apostolic traditions of the Church of England. 'Tractarianism', or the Oxford Movement, did not oppose liberalism through social reform or through 'high-church' ceremonial. It was a conservative, intellectual appeal to Anglican tradition. After twelve years it split, in 1845, when some of its leaders, including John Henry Newman (partly in reaction to low-church persecution, partly out of sheer intellectual conviction) decided that nothing separated them from Rome, and 'went over'. Although its enemies forecast otherwise, the Oxford Movement served to strengthen the spirit of Anglicanism both through devout laymen such as W. E. Gladstone and through its influence on religious education and architecture. The Broad Church, being posited on a more sociological appreciation of religion, was in difficulties when it appeared that less than a fifth of the English attended their parish church. The unique religious Census of 1851 showed that only about 35 per cent of the English population went to Sunday service, and—although there were intense regional variations here—half of these 'sat under' dissenting ministers. In 1848 and after the Broad Church Christian Socialists tried energetically to reach out to working men, but for every working man convinced by the theology of the group's leader, F. D. Maurice, ten were impressed by the novels of his colleague Charles Kingsley, and many more helped practically by the work of J. M. Ludlow for the trade unions and E. V. Neale for the infant co-operative movement.

Anglicans at least possessed a tradition, wealth, and breadth of manœuvre denied to the nonconformists. Sectionally divided and always treated with suspicion by the ruling classes, several of their leaders—notably Jabez Bunting of the Methodist Conference—tried to integrate themselves through their conservatism. Political radicalism tended to be the hallmark of rural or mining area Dissenters—the change in South Wales was particularly drastic—or of urban élites such as the Unitarians or the Quakers. Only in the 1850s, after the success of the Corn Law campaign, did dissent begin to flex its muscles, align itself with the Liberal Party, and demand either improvements in its own civic status or—in the programme of the 'Liberation Society' (founded in 1844)—the dismantling of the established Church. Organized dissent came to play a major—and troublesome—institutional role within Liberalism, but it was a wasting asset, as the steady trickle of wealthy nonconformists over to the Church of England showed.

In Scotland the controversy over patronage came to a head in the 'ten years' conflict' of 1833–43, which ended with the 'Disruption' of the established Kirk and the creation of a new independent 'Free Church'. The secular role of the Kirk rapidly crumbled—a statutory poor law was enacted in 1845—but religious politics continued to obsess the Scots middle class for the rest of the century.

'The ringing grooves of change'

The 1840s remained, however, a decade of crisis, even in terms of classical economics. British industry was still dominated by textiles, and the market for them was both finite and subject to increasing competition from America and Europe. The industry was overcapitalized, and the adoption of each new invention meant that the return on capital decreased; each commercial depression was steeper and longer lasting than the last. Real

wages increased only slowly, probably not sufficiently to coun-
ter the precipitate decline of the handwork trades and the high
marginal costs of urban life. To Karl Marx, surveying Britain
through the descriptions of his mill-owning friend Friedrich
Engels, this was all part of one pattern. Capitalism was doomed
to choke on its own surplus accumulations of capital; its increasingly underpaid labourers would, in the next economic
depression, rise decisively against it. He would have echoed
Shelley's challenge:

> Rise like Lions after slumber
> In unvanquishable number—
> Shake your chains to earth like dew
> Which in sleep had fallen on you—
> Ye are many—they are few.

In the 1840s events in Ireland seemed to bring the revolution
perceptibly nearer. The potato blight of 1845, 1846, and 1848
destroyed the basis of the country's population growth; between 1845 and 1850 up to a million died of the consequences
of malnutrition, two million emigrated between 1845 and 1855.
The poor Irish immigrant, prepared to work for wages far
below the English norm, had already been seen as an explosive
force; Carlyle had written in *Chartism* (1839):

Every man who will take the statistic spectacles off his nose, and look,
may discern in town or country . . . [that] the condition of the lower
multitude of English labourers approximates more and more to the
Irish competing with them in all markets. . . .

That this did not happen was substantially due to a dramatic
industrial development which simultaneously soaked up surplus
supplies of labour and capital and transformed them into a new
and more varied economy. Its principal—and psychologically
most spectacular—instrument was the railway.

  Railways of various primitive types had since the early seventeenth century carried coal from mine to port or river; by 1800
there were perhaps two hundred miles of horse-worked track

scattered throughout the country, built to various gauges and patterns, with wooden and later with iron rails. Cast iron was used from the 1770s, wrought iron 'edge-rail'—much more reliable—from the 1790s. Steam traction then appeared in two forms: stationary low-pressure engines dragged wagons up inclines, and light high-pressure 'locomotive' engines moved themselves on the rails. In 1804, Richard Trevithick demonstrated the locomotive in Wales, and it was soon adopted in the northern coalfield, where 'viewers' like George Stephenson were building large-capacity edge-railways whose demands stretched the capabilities of horse traction, as coal production doubled between 1800 and 1825. Throughout Britain by 1830, 375 miles of line, authorized by Parliament, had been built.

The commercial boom of the mid-1820s gave the next boost, with the promotion of the Liverpool and Manchester Railway. Cotton production had almost doubled between 1820 and 1830, and Manchester's population had risen by 47 per cent. Transport of the necessities for both was checked by the monopolistic Bridgewater Canal; a large-scale competitor was necessary. Its demands almost exceeded the technology available: only on the eve of its completion, and under pressure of an open competition, was an efficient enough locomotive produced by the Stephensons. The difference between the award-winning *Rocket* (1830) and the production-line *Patentee* (1834), however, was almost as great as that between the *Rocket* and its clumsy if reliable precursor, the *Locomotion*. Locomotive design did not subsequently change for half a century.

In the 1830s, railway development was buoyed up by another speculative boom. By 1840 nearly 2,400 miles of track connected London with Birmingham, Manchester, and Brighton. Some of the new lines were prosperous; others, overcapitalized and faced with penal land and legal charges, ran into trouble. There were few enough rules in the early days of joint-stock companies, and the reputation soared of those who succeeded in turning 'scrip into gold', such as George Hudson, 'the Railway King' who controlled a third of the system by 1845.

————	Before 1838
+++++	1838 — 48
————	1849 — 72
··········	1873 — 1914

Glasgow
Edinburgh
Berwick on Tweed
Newcastle upon Tyne
Carlisle
Stockton
Darlington
Lancaster
Leeds
York
Liverpool
Manchester
Doncaster
Holyhead
Crewe
Derby
Nottingham
Norwich
Birmingham
Peterboro
Rugby
Cambridge
Gloucester
Oxford
Swansea
Bristol
Swindon
London
Cardiff
Dover
Southampton
Exeter
Brighton
Weymouth
Portsmouth

0   50 miles
0   50   100 km

RAILWAYS IN THE NINETEENTH CENTURY 1825–1914

Hudson made his attractive profits by paying the dividends of existing lines with capital raised for new branches; when the great mania of the 1840s, which he helped promote, faltered in 1848, he was exposed and fled the country—but not before mileage had risen to over 8,000, and the network had been extended from Aberdeen to Plymouth.

But the railway age produced its heroes as well: the self-taught Stephenson and his brilliant son Robert, Joseph Locke, Daniel Gooch, and the polymath Isambard Kingdom Brunel, whose vast projects—the seven-foot-gauge Great Western Railway, the pioneer iron-and-screw steamer *Great Britain*, and the 18,000 ton sea-leviathan *Great Eastern*—fascinated the public as much as they terrified his unfortunate financial backers. 'What poet-race', G. K. Chesterton would later ask, 'shot such cyclopean arches at the stars?' Such men—Carlyle called them 'captains of industry'—were more attractive entrepreneurs than the cotton-masters, and Samuel Smiles was subsequently to make them paragons of 'self-help'.

This new transport system had been created in less than a score of years, and without any modern construction techniques. The 'navvies'—of whom 250,000 were said to be at work in 1848, powered by beer and beef—created the huge earthworks which characterized early British railways. The image of the British working man in the 1830s had been of the pathetic factory slave or starving cotton-weaver. In the 1850s it was provided by the brawny labourers who ran up the Crystal Palace in six months, and who were shipped to the Crimea to make good—with railways and camps—the incompetence of the military. The railways had cost an unprecedented amount of money, however: by 1849 no less than £224.6 million had been invested. In 1849 total receipts remained low at only £11.4 million; although they rose by 1859 to £24.4 million, railways were never more than a modest and reliable investment, and in the case of some companies they were far from that. Until 1852, they made more money from passengers than freight and the subsequent expansion of goods traffic was obtained to a great extent by a systematic process of buying over their chief competitors, the canals, whose owners, having hitherto enjoyed inflated profits, were little inclined to see themselves beggared by competition. By the mid-1850s, strategic sections of the canal network were in railway ownership, and traffics were ruthlessly transferred to rail. Already, in the most dynamic area of industrial growth, the conspiracy of capitalists denounced by Adam Smith had become a fact.

Politics and Diplomacy: Palmerston's Years

The railway boom coincided with a dramatic shift in politics. The harvests of 1842, 1843, and 1844 had been good; grain was plentiful and costs low. Then in 1845 the harvest was wrecked by bad weather, and the first blights hit the Irish potato crop. The arguments of the Anti-Corn Law League seemed confirmed. Peel attempted to carry free trade in Cabinet, failed, and resigned, only to come back when the Whigs could not form a ministry. In February 1846, he moved a package of measures abolishing duties on imported corn over three years. He thus bought—or hoped to buy—the support of the gentry through grants towards the poor law and local police forces. But his party was deeply split and only a minority supported him when he was censured on Irish coercion in May. In the ensuing election Russell came back with a Whig ministry, and Whigs and later Liberals dominated politics thereafter. Badly weakened by the shift of the Peelite élite, which included Gladstone, Aberdeen, and Sir James Graham, into the ambit of the Whigs, the Tory gentry now found themselves led by the ex-Whigs Lord Derby and Lord George Bentinck, and the exotic ex-radical Benjamin Disraeli. The Tories stood firm as a party, but held power for only five of the next thirty years.

There was a greater degree of party management, centred on the new clubs of St. James's, the Reform and the (Tory) Carlton, both founded in 1832, but to conceive of politics shading from left to right means imposing the criteria of a later age. National party organizations were as unknown as party programmes. Public speeches were rare. Leaders—still predominantly Whig magnates—would drop a few hints to their closest colleagues, often their relatives, about policy just before elections (which took place every seven years). Prospective candidates travelled to likely seats, issued addresses, and canvassed for the support of local notables, only 'going to the poll' if promised respectable support.

Huge expenses made contested elections the exception rather than the rule. The territorial nobility were impregnable in their many surviving 'pocket boroughs'. A vote—delivered in public—against, say, Blenheim Palace at Woodstock, was still an almost suicidal move for a local farmer or tradesman. Counties, likewise, were dominated by the great families. The medium-sized boroughs were more open but expensive; their electors sometimes reached the levels of corruption depicted at Eatanswill in Dickens's *Pickwick Papers*. The newly-enfranchised great towns could sometimes elect active if impecunious men—Macaulay sat for Leeds—but more often favoured affluent local businessmen, who usually bore most of the cost of the contest. Some things, however, remain familiar today: England was more conservative, the 'Celtic fringe' more radical.

Although Wellington's brief caretaker ministry of 1834 proved the last occasion on which a duke became first minister, power lay with the landed interest, in which the Whigs were still as well represented as the Tories, although in many cases the elevation to this status was recent, a tribute to the flexibility of the élite. Peel and Gladstone—both Oxford double-firsts—were only a generation removed from provincial industry and commerce, and even more remarkable was the rise of Benjamin Disraeli, adventurer and novelist, stemming from a religion whose members were only to obtain full civil equality in 1860.

Ministries spent little time over domestic legislation, but much more over foreign and service affairs—not surprisingly, since the latter claimed more than a third of the estimates. Neither navy nor army had changed much since 1815. The navy bought its first steamer, a tug called the *Monkey*, in 1822. With enormous reluctance, others were ordered in 1828, the Lords of the Admiralty feeling that 'the introduction of steam is calculated to strike a fatal blow at the supremacy of the Empire'. Paddles meant a loss of broadside guns, and sailing ships could keep station for years, so Devonport was still launching all-sail three-deckers in 1848, although the successful use of screw-propulsion on smaller ships was numbering the days of the sailing fleet. The old long-service army of about 130,000 men— 42 per cent Irish and 14 per cent Scots in 1830—poorly paid and wretchedly accommodated, kept the peace in Ireland and the colonies. In many small campaigns it advanced Britain's spheres of influence and trade in India, and in the 'Opium War' of 1839–42 in China, although now on behalf of free-trading merchants rather than the fading Chartered Companies.

Britain's withdrawal from European commitments was reflected, too, in her diplomacy. After the defeat of Napoleon, the Continental conservative leaders, above all Tsar Alexander I of Russia, tried to establish a system of co-operation in Europe through regular congresses of the great powers. But even in 1814 British diplomats preferred security to be achieved by the traditional means of the balance of power, even if this meant resurrecting France as a counterweight to Russia. For much of the time between then and 1848, a tacit Anglo-French *entente* subsisted, though it was disturbed in 1830 when Catholic Belgium detached itself from Holland, and looked as if it might fall into the French sphere of influence. The solution to this was found in Belgian neutrality, and a new royal family with close links with Britain—all guaranteed by the Treaty of London (1839), whose violation by Germany in August 1914 brought the long peace to an end.

Other problems between Britain and France were less easily settled, as they were linked with the steady decline of the Turkish Empire, which Britain wished to maintain as a buffer against Austria and Russia in the Balkans. For much of this period, the dominant figure was Palmerston, who, coming late into foreign affairs in 1830 at the age of forty-six, burrowed himself into the grubby premises of the Foreign Office in Whitehall (which at the zenith of its power had a staff of only forty-five) and stayed there as the dominant force for over thirty years—aggressively patriotic, but still, within limits, liberal. In 1847, however, the most celebrated British politician in Europe was not Palmerston but Cobden, the apostle of free trade. He was fêted in capital after capital, and his hosts were sure of one thing—the conservative monarchies were doomed, and the day of liberalism would shortly dawn.

Early in 1848, Marx and Engels drafted the *Communist Manifesto* in London, prophesying, on behalf of a small group of German socialists, a European revolution, to be led by the workers of those countries most advanced towards capitalism. Paris rose up against Louis Philippe on 24 February, then Berlin, Vienna, and the Italian states erupted. But Britain did not follow. There was a momentary panic when the Chartists brought their last great petition to London on 14 April; 10,000 special constables were sworn in; the telegraphs bought over for the week by the Home Office. The constables were potentially more worrying than the Chartists, as middle-class volunteer forces had spearheaded the Continental risings. But their loyalty was absolute; revolutions were something that happened elsewhere. The Chartists dispersed from Kennington Common; Parliament laughed the great petition out.

But there was no repetition of 1793 either. The republican government in Paris wanted to maintain co-operation with Britain, acted firmly against its own radicals, and did not try to export revolution. Palmerston wanted no change in the balance of power, but favoured constitutional regimes and an Austrian withdrawal from Italy. This moderation was scarcely successful, and Britain was unable to guarantee any of the gains that the liberals briefly made. A combination of peasant support bought by land reform and Russian aid, which crushed Hungary and gave Austria a free hand elsewhere, brought the *anciens régimes* back to power—but Austria was now prostrate and the Russians worryingly dominant in Eastern Europe.

Incorporation

Repeal of the Corn Law, the handling of the 1848 emergency, and the rapid expansion of the railways not only made the economic situation more hopeful but underpinned it with a new political consensus. The agricultural interest had been checked, but its farming efficiency enabled it to ride out foreign competition. At the same time the bourgeoisie realized that it had both to co-operate with the old élite in controlling the industrial workers, and to concede enough to the latter to stave off political explosions. In this context (particularly compared with textiles), railways, steamers, and telegraphs were all useful and glamorous, attractive advertisements for industrialization. Functionally, they brought together land, commerce, and industry. And they made lawyers in particular very rich.

By the 1850s the law 'incorporated' the working classes—or, at least, their leading members. The 'New Model' trade unions of skilled workers, such as the Engineers and the Carpenters, pressed not for drastic state intervention but for contractual equality. They acted not through public demonstrations but through diplomatic pressure on MPs of both parties. Their procedures and iconography rejected the oaths and mysticism of the old quasi-conspiratorial societies for an almost pedantic legalism, concerned with defending their respectability at the top of the working class.

Economic and social theory moved towards the idea of 'incorporation'. Classical economics had earlier been subversive and pessimistic: one strand of it, in the hands of Marx, remained so. But John Stuart Mill in his *Logic* of 1840 and his *Political Economy* of 1848 reconciled utilitarianism with gradual reform and sympathy for the aims of moderate working-class leaders. Mill found to his surprise that the *Logic*, with its substantial borrowings from the French sociological tradition of Saint-Simon and Auguste Comte, became the orthodoxy of the older universities, which were recuperating from the traumas of the Oxford Movement. But the 'Saint of Rationalism' himself had, in his enthusiasm for the English Romantic poets, gone far to make his blend of utilitarianism, ethical individualism, and reformist 'socialism' acceptable to reformers within the establishment, who broadcast it in the high-minded literary reviews which burgeoned around the mid-century.

In the eyes of the candidates for political incorporation, 'the rule of law' was far from absolute. A. V. Dicey, who applied the phrase to nineteenth-century government, was himself to write in the 1860s: 'John Smith *qua* John Smith cannot be suppressed, but John Smith *qua* artisan can.' But he expected that the extension of the franchise would end such inequities. As, by and large, it did.

Who then remained 'without the law'? The Irish had been wounded too deeply. 'Repeal of the Union' was O'Connell's bequest to a new generation of patriots. Although the Catholic middle class, like the Scots, proved anxious to find niches in the British establishment, Irish nationalists were made more aggressive by the famine, and could in the future count on the aid of their embittered emigrant brethren in America. Settlers in the colonies may have prided themselves on their transplanting of British institutions, but as the Colonial Office was aware, settler notions of law found no place for the rights of the natives. High and low churchmen complained when the courts upheld the vague and all-embracing formulas of the Broad Church establishment. They could not dislodge it but they could indelibly affect the skyline of Victorian cities and the practice of piety.

The intellectuals accepted the notion of political and social evolution—Tennyson's 'freedom slowly broadens down/from precedent to precedent'—long before Darwin's *Origin of Species* appeared in 1859. Although no friend to liberalism, Thomas Carlyle's commendations of self-reliance and the work ethic gave individualism an almost religious quality. John Stuart Mill became a pillar of the mid-Victorian Liberal Party, eccentric only in his desire to extend 'incorporation' to the half of the population whom politics ignored—women (whose slow progress to civic and legal equality started, however, to accelerate during the 1850s). Two more troubled intellects were difficult to pin down. John Ruskin, 'the graduate of Oxford' whose *Modern Painters* was the sensation of 1843, combined reverence for aristocracy with increasingly subversive views on the economy and the environment; though his directly political impact was to be minimal compared to that of Robert Owen. No one savaged the law's delays and inequities more energetically than Charles Dickens, yet no one worried more about the results of revolution and lawlessness. The Circumlocution Office, the Tite Barnacles, Jarndyce *versus* Jarndyce, were balanced by Slackbridge, Madame Defarge, and Bill Sikes, though Dicey got it just about right when, on balance, he put Dickens alongside Shaftesbury as a force pushing public opinion towards 'positive' reforming legislation.

Militant dissent and old radicalism had their own worldview, remote from that of the establishment, but its tentacles reached out towards them. The middle class read 'industrial novels,' such as Disraeli's *Sybil*, in the 1840s, anxious about and intrigued by conditions in the great towns, trying to personalize their problems and reconcile them with individualist morality. But Mrs Gaskell in *Mary Barton* and Charles Kingsley in *Alton Locke* could not provide any such assurance; the only effective solution for their most heroic characters was emigration. Dickens's savage Carlylean satire on Manchester, *Hard Times*, wavered and collapsed when it came to considering any better future for the inhabitants of Coketown.

But few of the Coketown people had time or money to read about what the literati thought of their plight, and little enough was known about what they read, although it was obviously affected by the co-option of the literary radicals by a middle-class public. Henry Mayhew, the pioneer social investigator of the *Morning Chronicle*, just about carried on the journalistic tradition of Cobbett and Hazlitt into the 1860s; Dickens, from the same Bohemian milieu, shifted away from it. We know that the 'labour aristocracy' in the trade unions read what their betters wanted them to read; that the religious kept their Bibles and their *Pilgrim's Progress*; but what of the 'roughs', and 'tavern society'? A folk tradition survived and developed in the fishing ports, among the weavers, and on the farms. Later in the nineteenth century, an American professor discovered two-thirds of the great traditional English ballads still being sung in the 'Farmtouns' of north-east Scotland, where the more plebeian 'bothy ballads' acted as a means of spreading information about farmers among the ploughmen and carters, and the 'Society of the Horseman's Word' conserved a primitive, but effective, trade unionism.

In his novel *Except the Lord* (1953) about the mid-Victorian youth of a radical politician, Joyce Cary takes his hero, Chester Nimmo, into a fairground tent. A troupe of actors are performing *Maria Marten, or the Murder in the Red Barn*, a staple of nineteenth-century melodrama, loosely based on an actual murder which occurred in 1830—the eve of 'Captain Swing'. This was Nimmo's reaction:

The drama that we saw, and that millions had seen, was a story of the cruellest hurt of many inflicted by the rich on the poor. Throughout the play everything possible was done to show the virtue, innocence and helplessness of the poor, and the abandoned cruelty, the heartless self-indulgence of the rich.

And this was one among hundreds of such plays. I have wondered often how such propaganda failed to bring to England also, as to France, Italy, Germany, almost every other nation, a bloody revolution, for its power was incredible. As I say, it was decisive in my own life . . .

Cary, a subtle and historically aware novelist, seems to have sensed here a resentment and grievance deep enough to be concealed by the respectability and self-help of formal working-class politics but for which political 'incorporation', the repetitive rows of sanitarily adequate workmen's dwellings, the increasingly opulent chapels, the still-locked Sunday parks, offered no consolation.

FURTHER READING

1. THE EIGHTEENTH CENTURY

GENERAL WORKS

J. R. Jones, *Country and Court: England, 1658–1714* (London, 1978);
W. A. Speck, *Stability and Strife: England, 1714–1760* (London, 1977);
I. R. Christie, *Wars and Revolutions: Britain 1760–1815* (London, 1982): three books in Arnold's *New History of England* which together provide a general survey of the period.

J. B. Owen, *The Eighteenth Century, 1714–1815* (London, 1974), one of the more recent and most useful of the many outline histories of the eighteenth century.

POLITICS

J. H. Plumb, *The Growth of Political Stability in England 1675–1725* (London, 1967), one of the most influential studies.

J. Cannon (ed.), *The Whig Ascendancy: Colloquies on Hanoverian England* (London, 1981), discusses the recent literature on stability and on many other themes.

H. T. Dickinson, *Politics and Literature in the Eighteenth Century* (London, 1974), includes representative selections from contemporary works.

—— *Liberty and Property: Political Ideology in Eighteenth-Century Britain* (London, 1977), a useful account for those interested in the history of ideas.

J. Cannon, *Parliamentary Reform 1640–1832* (Cambridge, 1973, rev. edn. 1982), deals with a particularly important theme.

J. R. Jones, *Britain and the World 1649–1815* (London, 1980), describes international relations in a British context.

I. R. Christie and B. W. Labaree, *Empire or Independence 1760–1776* (London, 1976);

P. J. Marshall, *Problems of Empire: Britain and India 1757–1813* (London, 1968); discussions of two particularly important imperial problems, America and India, respectively.

L. Namier, *The Structure of Politics at the Accession of George III* (London, 1967).

P. G. M. Dickson, *The Financial Revolution in England* (London, 1967).

ECONOMIC AND SOCIAL

E. Pawson, *The Early Industrial Revolution: Britain in the Eighteenth Century* (London, 1979), a useful addition to the many economic history textbooks on the eighteenth century.

R. Porter, *English Society in the Eighteenth Century* (London, 1982), presents a colourful picture of social conditions, opportunities, and developments.

G. E. Mingay, *English Landed Society in the Eighteenth Century* (London, 1963), deals with the gentry.

R. W. Malcolmson, *Life and Labour in England 1700–1780* (London, 1981), deals with the lower orders.

J. Stevenson, *Popular Disturbances in England 1700–1870* (London, 1979), also useful on popular politics.

P. Corfield, *The Impact of English Towns 1700–1800* (Oxford, 1982), a survey of eighteenth-century urban growth.

D. Hay, P. Linebaugh, E. P. Thompson, *Albion's Fatal Tree: Crime and Society in Eighteenth Century England* (London, 1975), a pioneering study in the now flourishing history of crime.

J. Cannon, *Aristocratic Century: The Peerage of Eighteenth-Century England* (Cambridge, 1984), argues for aristocratic dominance of the period.

N. McKendrick, J. Brewer, and J. H. Plumb, *The Birth of a Consumer Society: The Commercialisation of Eighteenth-Century England* (London, 1982).

M. D. George, *London Life in the Eighteenth Century* (London, 1925), a classic of social and urban history.

P. Deane, *The First Industrial Revolution* (Cambridge, 1965), remains the best analytical introduction to its subject.

J. D. Chambers and G. E. Mingay, *The Agricultural Revolution 1750–1880* (London, 1966).

J. M. Beattie, *Crime and the Courts in England, 1660–1800* (Oxford, 1986), provides a definitive study of the operations of the criminal law.

RELIGIOUS AND CULTURAL

M. R. Watts, *The Dissenters: From the Reformation to the French Revolution* (Oxford, 1978).

N. Sykes, *Church and State in England in the Eighteenth Century* (London, 1932).

J. Redwood, *Reason, Ridicule and Religion: The Age of Enlightenment in England, 1660–1750* (London, 1976).

A. Armstrong, *The Church of England, the Methodists and Society 1700–1850* (London, 1973), a brief summary of the religious history of the period.

R. Paulson, *Emblem and Expression: Meaning in English Art of the Eighteenth Century* (London, 1975), transmits something of the flavour as well as some of the most important aspects of cultural controversy.

The English Satirical Print 1600–1823 in seven volumes (Cambridge, 1986), reproduces a wealth of contemporary cartoons and illustrations on diverse aspects of the age.

2. REVOLUTION AND THE RULE OF LAW

GENERAL

Elie Halévy, *England in 1815* (Paris, 1913, London, 1924), an early but still authoritative account.

G. M. Young, *Victorian England: the Portrait of an Age* (Oxford, 1936), a key reappraisal, rescuing the nineteenth century from the likes of Lytton Strachey.

J. Steven Watson, *The Reign of George III, 1760–1815* (Oxford, 1960).

E. L. Woodward, *The Age of Reform, 1815–70* (Oxford, 1960).

G. S. Kitson Clark, *The Making of Victorian England* (London, 1962), like G. M. Young a high Tory, but unusually sensitive to the nature of middle-class reforming movements.

J. F. C. Harrison, *Early Victorian England, 1835–1850* (London, 1973), particularly strong on protest and radical movements.

C. Cook and Brian Keith, *British Historical Facts, 1830–1900* (London, 1975), includes economic as well as election and ministerial data.

ECONOMIC

Paul Mantoux, *The Industrial Revolution of the Eighteenth Century* (1911, London, 1961), pioneer and still perceptive study by a French historian.

J. H. Clapham, *An Economic History of Modern Britain* (Cambridge, 1933), some of Clapham's conclusions—notably over the standard of living—must be revised, but still conveys a wealth of detailed information. Best used as a supplement to Peter Mathias.

Peter Mathias, *The First Industrial Nation* (2nd rev. edn. London, 1983), reasonably up-to-date synthesis.

François Crouzet, *The Victorian Economy* (London, 1982), a synthesis of recent research by the leading French authority on the British economy.

Michael Robbins, *The Railway Age* (London, 1962), thematic study of railways and society.

Charles Hadfield, *British Canals* (London, 1950), an introduction to his great series of regional histories.

L. T. C. Rolt, *Victorian Engineering* (Harmondsworth, 1970), stress on mechanical engineering.

R. J. Morris and John Langton (eds.), *Atlas of Industrializing Britain* (London, 1986).

POLITICS AND GOVERNMENT

Oliver MacDonagh, *A Pattern of Government Growth* (London, 1961), a study of passenger ship regulation as an example of administrative development.

Michael Brock, *The Great Reform Bill* (London, 1973), the 1832 Reform Act.

E. J. Hobsbawm and George Rudé, *Captain Swing* (London, 1968), the labourers' revolts of 1831.

S. E. Finer, *Edwin Chadwick* (London, 1952), study of the great Benthamite reformer.

Norman McCord, *The Anti-Corn-Law League* (London, 1975).

Asa Briggs (ed.), *Chartist Studies* (London, 1974), emphasizes geographical diversity of movement.

Beatrice and Sidney Webb, *The History of Local English Government* (London, 1908–29).

Jasper Ridley, *Palmerston* (London, 1970).

A. V. Dicey, *The Relation between Law and Public Opinion in England in the Nineteenth Century* (London, 1906), lucid, influential but simplistic approach.

Dorothy Thompson, *The Chartists* (Aldershot, 1986).

SOCIETY

J. F. C. Harrison, *Robert Owen and the Owenites* (London, 1969).

Clive Emsley, *British Society and the French Wars, 1793–1815* (London, 1979), draws on much untapped archive material.

E. P. Thompson, *The Making of the English Working Class* (London, 1963), a controversial masterpiece.

—— *Whigs and Hunters* (London, 1975), law and society in the eighteenth century.

Harold Perkin, *The Origins of Modern English Society, 1780–1880* (London, 1969).

Roy Porter, *English Society in the 18th Century* (Harmondsworth, 1982).

W. R. Ward, *Religious Society in England, 1790–1950* (London, 1972), changes in family organization, mores, and emotions.

Lawrence Stone, *The Family, Sex and Marriage, 1500–1800* (London, 1977), changes in family organization, mores, and emotions.

Brian Simon, *Studies in the History of Education, 1780–1870* (London, 1960), strong on nonconformity and educational innovation.

Owen Chadwick, *The Victorian Church* (3rd edn. London, 1971), definitive; despite title, deals with all the churches.

Donald Read, *The English Provinces* (London, 1964), social background to industrial revolution and Anti-Corn Law League.

John Foster, *The Class Struggle in the Industrial Revolution* (London, 1974), well-researched Marxist interpretation of industry and politics in South Shields, Northampton, and Oldham.

Lawrence and Jeanne C. Fawtier Stone, *An Open Elite? England 1540–1880* (Oxford, 1984).

SCOTLAND, IRELAND, WALES

T. C. Smout, *A History of the Scottish People* (London, 1969).

—— *A Century of the Scottish People, 1830–1950* (London, 1986).

E. D. Evans, *A History of Wales, 1600–1815* (Cardiff, 1976).

Gearóid O'Tuathaigh, *Ireland before the Famine, 1798–1848* (Dublin, 1972).

CULTURE

Francis D. Klingender, *Art and the Industrial Revolution* (London, 1972), Marxist interpretation of art and industry, from optimism to doubt, *c.*1750–1850.

Raymond Williams, *Culture and Society*, *1780–1950* (London, 1958), study of the social critical condition: Burke, Cobbett, Carlyle, Ruskin.

CHRONOLOGY

* Entries in *italics* denote events belonging to the history of the Roman Empire.

407	Constantine III proclaimed in Britain
	Constantine III rules from Arles (407–11)
409	Britain revolts from Constantine III: end of Roman rule in Britain
410	'Rescript of Honorius': letter to Britons (?), significance disputed
429	St. Germanus visits Britain
c.450	The *adventus Saxonum*: Hengest and Horsa settle in Kent (traditional date)
455	Hengest rebels against Vortigern (traditional date)
477	Saxon settlement of Sussex (traditional date)
495	Saxon settlement of Wessex (traditional date)
c.500	Battle of *Mons Badonicus*
560	Æthelberht, later over-king, becomes king in Kent
577	The West Saxons capture Gloucester, Cirencester and Bath
597	St. Augustine's mission arrives in Kent
616	Raedwald of East Anglia, as over-king, makes Edwin king of Northumbria
c.624	Death of Raedwald, and his probable burial in the Sutton Hoo barrow
627	Conversion of Edwin and the Northumbrian court
633	Battle of Heavenfield; Oswald of Northumbria becomes over-king
635	Conversion of King Cynegils of Wessex
642	Oswald is killed at Oswestry by King Penda of Mercia
655	Penda is defeated and killed at the *Winwaed* by Oswy of Northumbria, who becomes over-king
664	Synod of Whitby
669	Arrival of Archbishop Theodore
672	Synod of Hertford; battle of the Trent, marking the beginnings of the rise of Mercia
685–8	Expansion of Wessex under Caedwalla to include Kent, Surrey and Sussex
716	Æthelbald become king of Mercia
731	Bede completes his *Ecclesiastical History*
746–7	First Council of Clofesho
757	Death of Æthelbald; Offa becomes king of Mercia
786	Legatine Council held under Offa

793–5	Danish raids on Lindisfarne, Jarrow, and Iona
796	Death of Offa
825	Egbert of Wessex defeats Mercia and annexes Kent, Essex, Surrey, and Sussex
835	Big Danish raid on Kent
865	The Danish 'Great Army' lands
867	Northumbria falls to the Danes
870	East Anglia falls to the Danes; murder of St. Edmund
871	The Danes attack Wessex; Alfred becomes king
874	Mercia falls to the Danes
878	(March) The Danes drive Alfred into the Somerset marshes
	(May) Alfred defeats the Danes at Edington; Guthrum is baptized
899	Death of Alfred; Edward 'the Elder' becomes king of Wessex
910–20	Edward and Æthelflaed reconquer most of the Danelaw
919	Norse kingdom of York is founded by Raegnald
924	Death of Edward; Athelstan becomes king
937	Athelstan defeats the Norse, Scots and Strathclyde Welsh at Brunanburh
939	Death of Athelstan; Edmund become king
940	Dunstan begin to refound Glastonbury as a regular monastic house
946	Death of Edmund
954	The last king of York is deposed
959	Edgar becomes king
960	Dunstan becomes Archbishop of Canterbury
c.970	*Regularis Concordia* is compiled
973	Edgar is crowned and consecrated, and receives the submission of British princes
975	Death of Edgar; Edward 'the Martyr' becomes king
979	Murder of Edward; Æthelred 'the Unready' becomes king
991	The Danes defeat Alderman Byrhtnoth and the Essex levies at Maldon; treaty between England and Normandy
1002	Æthelred orders the massacre of all Danes in England

1003	Danish invasion led by King Swein
1013	Swein returns with a new army; the Danelaw accepts him as king
1014	Swein dies; the Danish army in England elect Cnut as their king
1016	(April) Æthelred dies; Edmund 'Ironside' becomes king
	(autumn) Cnut defeats Edmund at Ashingdon; Edmund dies and Cnut becomes King of all England
1017	Cnut divides England into four earldoms
1035	Death of Cnut
1037	Harold becomes king
1040	Death of Harold; Harthacnut becomes king
1042	Death of Harthacnut; Edward 'the Confessor' becomes king
1051–2	Conflict between King Edward and Godwin earl of Wessex
1053	Death of Godwin; his son Harold becomes earl of Wessex
1064–5	Earl Harold visits Duke William in Normandy
1066	(January) Death of King Edward; Earl Harold becomes king
	(September) King Harold of England defeats and kills King Harold of Norway at Stamford Bridge
	(October) Duke William of Normandy defeats and kills King Harold of England at Hastings

VOL. 2 THE MIDDLE AGES

1066	(December) William is consecrated king
1067–70	English rebellions
1069–70	The harrying of the north
1086	Domesday Survey carried out
1087	Death of William I; accession of William II Rufus
1088	Rebellion in support of Robert Curthose
1093	Anselm appointed Archbishop of Canterbury
1096	Robert pawns Normandy ot Rufus
1100	Death of William Rufus; accession of Henry I
1101	Invasion of Robert Curthose
1106	Battle of Tinchebray; Curthose imprisoned; Henry I takes Normandy
1107	Settlement of Investiture Dispute in England

1120	Wreck of the White Ship
1128	Marriage of Empress Matilda to Geoffrey of Anjou
1135	Death of Henry I; accession of Stephen
1139–53	Civil war in England
1141	Battle of Lincoln; Stephen captured; later exchanged for Robert of Gloucester
1141–5	Geoffrey of Anjou conquers Normandy
1149	Cession of Northumbria to David of Scotland
1152	Henry of Anjou (later Henry II) marries Eleanor of Aquitaine
1153	Henry invades England; he and Stephen come to terms
1154	Death of Stephen; accession of Henry II
1157	Henry regains Northumbria
1162	Becket appointed Archbishop of Canterbury
1164	Council and Constitutions of Clarendon; Becket goes into exile
1166	Assize of Clarendon
1169–72	English conquest of Ireland begins
1170	Coronation of the young king; murder of Becket
1173–4	Rebellion against Henry II; William 'the Lion' (king of Scotland) invades the north
1183	Death of the young king
1189	Death of Henry II; accession of Richard I
1190–92	Richard I on crusade
1193–4	Richard in prison in Germany
1193–1205	Hubert Walter, Archbishop of Canterbury (justiciar 1194–8; chancellor 1199–1205)
1197	Death of Rhys of Deheubarth
1199	Death of Richard I; accession of John; establishment of Chancery Rolls
1203–4	Philip Augustus conquers Anjou and Normandy
1208–14	Interdict in England
1214	Battle of Bouvines: French victory
1215	Magna Carta; civil war in England
1216	Louis (later Louis VIII) invades; death of John; accession of Henry III
1217	Battles of Lincoln and Dover; Louis withdraws
1221–4	Arrival of Dominican and Franciscan Friars in England
1224	Louis VIII completes conquest of Poitou

1232	Dismissal of Hubert de Burgh
1240	Death of Llywelyn the Great
1254	Henry III accepts papal offer of throne of Sicily
1258	Barons take over royal government; provisions of Oxford
1259	Treaty of Paris between England and France
1264	Battle of Lewes; Henry III captured; government of Simon de Montfort
1265	Battle of Evesham; killing of Simon de Montfort
1267	Henry recognizes Llywelyn ap Gruffydd as Prince of Wales
1272	Death of Henry III; accession of Edward I
1276–7	First Welsh War
1282–3	Edward's conquest of Wales
1286–9	Edward I in Gascony
1291	Edward I asserts his overlordship over Scotland
1294	War with France begins
1295	Franco-Scottish alliance
1296	Edward I invades Scotland; his conflict with the Church
1297	Edward I's conflict with his magnates; his expedition to Flanders
1306	Rebellion of Robert Bruce
1307	Death of Edward I; accession of Edward II
1314	Scottish victory at Bannockburn
1315–16	Great famine
1321–2	Civil war in England
1327	Deposition and death of Edward II; accession of Edward III
1330	Edward III takes the reins of government
1337	The Hundred Years War begins
1339–41	Political crisis in England
1346	English victories at Crécy and Neville's Cross
1347	English capture Calais
1348	First occurrence of plague in England
1356	English victory at Poitiers
1361	Second major occurrence of plague
1376	'Good Parliament' meets; death of Edward, the Black Prince
1377	Death of Edward III; accession of Richard II

1381	The Peasants' Revolt
1382	Condemnation of John Wycliffe's works
1388	'Merciless Parliament' meets; battle of Otterburn against the Scots
1389	Richard II declares himself of age
1394–5	Richard II's expedition to Ireland
1396	Anglo-French treaty
1397–9	Richard II's 'tyranny'
1399	Deposition of Richard II; accession of Henry IV
1400	Rebellion of Owain Glyndŵr begins (to 1410)
1403	Henry Hotspur defeated at Shrewsbury
1405	Execution of Archbishop Scrope of York
1408	Defeat of the earl of Northumberland at Bramham Moor
1413	Death of Henry IV; accession of Henry V
1415	English victory at Agincourt
1419–20	English conquest of Normandy
1420	Anglo-French treaty of Troyes
1422	Death of Henry V; accession of Henry VI
1435	Death of John, duke of Bedford; Franco-Burgundian treaty of Arras
1436–7	Henry VI comes of age
1445	Henry VI marries Margaret of Anjou
1449–50	French overrun Normandy
1450	Murder of the duke of Suffolk; John Cade's rebellion
1453	French overrun Gascony; Henry VI becomes ill
1455	Battle of St. Albans between Richard, duke of York and the royalist forces
1459	Defeat of the duke of York at Blore Heath and Ludford Bridge
1461	Deposition of Henry VI; accession of Edward IV
1465	Capture of Henry VI
1469	Rebellion of Richard, earl of Warwick and George, duke of Clarence
1470	Deposition of Edward IV; return of Henry VI
1471	Return of Edward IV; death of the earl of Warwick at Barnet; death of Henry VI
1475	Edward IV's expedition to France; Anglo-French treaty of Picquigny

1477	William Caxton's first printed book in England
1483	Death of Edward IV; accession, deposition, and death of Edward V; accession of Richard III; rebellion of Henry, duke of Buckingham
1485	Death of Richard III at Bosworth; accession of Henry VII

VOL. 3 THE TUDORS AND STUARTS

1487	Rebellion of Lambert Simnel
1491	Birth of Prince Henry
1509	Accession of Henry VIII
1510	Execution of Empson and Dudley
1512	War with France and Scotland
1513	Battle of Flodden: English victory over Scotland
1515	Wolsey appointed Lord Chancellor
1522	War with France
1525	Peace with France
1527	Divorce crisis begins
1528	War with Spain
1529	Peace of Cambrai; fall of Wolsey: Sir Thomas More succeeds as Lord Chancellor
1532	More resigns
1533	Henry VIII marries Anne Boleyn; Act of Appeals; birth of Princess Elizabeth
1534	Act of Supremacy
1535	Execution of More and Fisher
1536	Dissolution of the Monasteries; Pilgrimage of Grace; union of England and Wales
1542	Battle of Solway Moss; English victory over invading Scottish army
1543	War with France
1547	Succession of Edward VI; ascendancy of Protector Somerset; battle of Pinkie: English victory over Scotland
1549	First Book of Common Prayer; Northumberland's coup
1553	Accession of Mary
1554	Pole returns; reunion with Rome; Wyatt's rebellion
1555	Persecution of Protestants begins
1557	War with France

1558	New Book of Rates; accession of Elizabeth I
1559	Peace of Cateau-Cambrésis; religious Settlement in England
1566	Archbishop Parker's *Advertisements* demand religious conformity
1568	Mary Stuart flees to England
1569	Northern Rebellion
1570	Papal bull declares Elizabeth excommunicated and deposed
1580	Jesuit missionaries arrive in England
1585	War with Spain
1587	Execution of Mary Stuart
1588	Defeat of the Spanish Armada
1594	Bad harvests begin
1601	Essex's rebellion
1603	Death of Elizabeth; accession of James VI of Scotland as James I; peace in Ireland; Millenary Petition of the Puritans
1604	Peace with Spain (treaty of London); Hampton Court Conference (king, bishops, Puritans)
1605	Gunpowder Plot, the last major Catholic conspiracy
1606–7	Failure of James's plans for union of kingdoms
1607	Settlement of Virginia
1609	Rebellion of the Northern Earls in Ireland; beginnings of the Planting of Ulster by Scots and English Protestants
1610	Failure of Great Contract (reform of royal finance)
1611	Publication of Authorized Version of the Bible (Anglican–Puritan co-operation)
1612	Death of Prince Henry, James's promising elder son
1613	Marriage of Princess Elizabeth to Elector Palatine, Protestant zealot, enmeshed Britain in continental politics
1617–29	Ascendancy of George Villiers, duke of Buckingham
1919–22	Inigo Jones designs the Banqueting House, the first major royal public building since the reign of Henry VIII
1620	Pilgrim Fathers inaugurate religious migration to New England

1622–3	Prince Charles and Buckingham go to Spain to woo the king's daughter and are rebuffed
1624–30	War with Spain
1625	Death of James I; accession of Charles I and marriage to Henrietta Maria, sister of Louis XIII of France
1626–9	War with France
1628	Petition of Right; publication of Harvey's work on the circulation of the blood; assassination of Buckingham
1629	Charles I dissolves Parliament, determines to govern without one
1630	Large-scale emigration to Massachusetts begins
1633	William Laud translated to be Archbishop of Canterbury
1634–40	Ship Money case
1637	Hampden's case supports Charles I's claim to collect Ship Money
1637–40	Breakdown of Charles's government of Scotland and two attempts to impose his will by force
1640	Long Parliament summoned
1641	Remodelling of government in England and Scotland; abolition of conciliar courts, abolition of prerogative taxation, triennial bill, Grand Remonstrance; rebellion of Ulster Catholics
1642	King's attempt on the Five Members; his withdrawal from London; the 19 Propositions; the resort of arms: Civil War
1643	King's armies prosper; Scots invade on side of Parliament
1644	Parliamentary armies prosper, especially in the decisive battle of the war, Marston Moor (June)
1645	'Clubmen' risings of armed neutrals threaten both sides; Royalist armies disintegrate, but parliamentary forces reorganized (New Model Army)
1646	King surrenders to the Scots; bishops and Book of Common Prayer abolished, Presbyterian Church established
1647	Army revolt; radical movements criticize parliamentary tyranny; king prevaricates

1648	Second Civil War: Scots now side with the king and are defeated; provincial risings (Kent, Colchester, South Wales, Yorks., etc.) crushed
1649	Trial and execution of Charles I: England a Republic
1649–53	Government by sovereign single-chamber assembly, the 'Rump' Parliament thoroughly purged of royalists and moderates
1649–50	Oliver Cromwell conquers Ireland (Drogheda massacre)
1650–2	Oliver Cromwell conquers Scotland (battles of Dunbar and Worcester)
1651	Thomas Hobbes's *Leviathan* published
1652–4	First Dutch War
1653	Cromwell dissolves Rump, creates the Nominated or Barebones Assembly; it surrenders power back to him, and he becomes Lord Protector under a paper constitution (*The Instrument of Government*)
1655–60	War with Spain
1655	Royalist insurrection (Penruddock's rising) is a complete failure
1657	*Instrument of Government* replaced by a parliamentary paper constitution, the *Humble Petition and Advice*; Cromwell rejects title of King and remains Lord Protector, but nominates his own House of Lords
1658	Cromwell dies and is succeeded by his son Richard
1659	Richard overthrown by the army; Rump restored but displeases many in the army
1660	Charles II restored
1662	Church of England restored; Royal Society receives its Charter
1663	Failure of first royal attempt to grant religious toleration
1665–7	Second Dutch War
1665	Great Plague (final major outbreak)
1666	Great Fire of London
1667	Milton's *Paradise Lost* published
1672–3	Failure of second royal attempt to grant religious toleration
1672–4	Third Dutch War

1674	Grain bounties introduced (England self-sufficient in food)
1678	Titus Oates and the Popish Plot; Bunyan's *Pilgrim's Progress*, part I, published
1679–81	The Exclusion Crisis; emergence of Whig and Tory parties
1683	The Rye House Plot; Whigs proscribed
1685	Charles II dies; accession of James II; rebellion by Charles II's protestant bastard, the duke of Monmouth, fails
1687	James II's Declaration of Indulgence; Tories proscribed; Newton's *Principia Mathematica* published
1688	James II's son born
1688	William of Orange invades: James II takes flight, accession of William III (of Orange) and Mary

VOL. 4 THE EIGHTEENTH CENTURY AND THE AGE OF INDUSTRY

1689	Bill of Rights settles succession to the throne and declares illegal various grievances; Toleration Act grants rights to Trinitarian Protestant dissenters
1690	Battle of the Boyne: William III defeats Irish and French army
1694	Bank of England founded; death of Queen Mary; Triennial Act sets the maximum duration of a parliament at three years
1695	Lapse of Licensing Act
1697	Peace treaty of Ryswick between allied powers of the League of Augsburg and France; Civil List Act votes funds for the maintenance of the royal household
1701	War of Spanish Succession begins; Act of Settlement settles the royal succession on the descendants of Sophia of Hanover
1702	Death of William III; accession of Anne
1704	Battle of Blenheim: British, Dutch, German and Austrian troops defeat French and Bavarian forces; British capture of Gibraltar from Spain
1707	Union of England and Scotland
1710	Impeachment of Dr Sacheverell; Harley ministry
1713	Peace treaty of Utrecht concludes the War of Spanish Succession

1714	Death of Anne; accession of George I
1715	Jacobite rebellion aimed at overthrowing the Hanoverian succession fails
1716	Septennial Act sets the maximum duration of a parliament at seven years
1717	Whig split; suspension of convocation
1720	South Sea Bubble: many investors ruined after speculation in the stock of the South Sea Company
1721	Walpole ministry
1722	Atterbury Plot, the most notable Jacobite plot
1726	Jonathan Swift's *Gulliver's Travels* published
1727	Death of George I; accession of George II
1729	Alexander Pope's *Dunciad* published
1730	Walpole/Townshend split
1733	Excise crisis: Walpole has to abandon his plans to reorganize the customs and excise
1737	Death of Queen Caroline
1738	Wesley's 'conversion': the start of Methodism
1739	War of Jenkins' Ear: Anglo-Spanish naval war
1740	War of the Austrian Succession
1741	Samuel Richardson's *Pamela* published
1742	Fall of Walpole
1744	Ministry of Pelham
1745	Jacobite Rebellion led by 'Bonnie Prince Charlie'
1746	Battle of Culloden: the duke of Cumberland routs the Jacobite army
1748	Peace of Aix-la-Chapelle concludes War of the Austrian Succession
1752	Adoption of Gregorian Calendar
1753	Jewish Naturalization Bill
1754	Newcastle ministry
1756	Seven Years War: Britain allied with Frederick the Great of Prussian against France, Austria, and Russia
1757	Pitt–Newcastle ministry; battle of Plassey: British victory over Bengal
1759	Capture of Quebec: British victory over the French
1760	Death of George II; accession of George III
1761	Laurence Sterne's *Tristram Shandy* published
1762	Bute's ministry
1763	Peace of Paris concludes Seven Years War; Grenville

	ministry; Wilkes and General Warrants
1765	Rockingham ministry; American Stamp Act attempts to make the defence of the American colonies self-financing: repealed 1766
1766	Chatham ministry
1768	Grafton ministry; Middlesex election crisis
1769	James Watt's steam engine patented
1770	Lord North's ministry; Edmund Burke's *Thoughts on the Present Discontents* published; Falkland Islands crisis
1773	Boston Tea Party: American colonists protest against the East India Company's monopoly of tea exports to America
1774	Coercive Acts passed in retaliation for Boston Tea Party
1776	Declaration of American Independence; Edward Gibbon's *Decline and Fall* and Adam Smith's *Wealth of Nations* published
1779	Wyvill's Association movement
1780	Gordon Riots develop from a procession to petition parliament against the Catholic Relief Act
1781	Surrender at Yorktown: American victory over British troops
1782	Second Rockingham ministry
1783	Shelburne ministry; Peace of Versailles recognizes independence of American colonies; Fox–North coalition; Younger Pitt's ministry
1784	East India Act
1785	Pitt's motion for parliamentary reform defeated
1786	Eden commercial treaty with France
1789	French Revolution
1790	Edmund Burke's *Reflections on the Revolution in France* published
1791	Thomas Paine's *The Rights of Man* published
1792	Coal gas used for lighting; Mary Wollstonecraft's *Vindication of the Rights of Women* published
1793	Outbreak of war with France; voluntary Board of Agriculture set up; commercial depression
1795	'Speenhamland' system of outdoor relief adopted, making up wages to equal cost of subsistence

1796	Vaccination against smallpox introduced
1798	T. R. Malthus's *Essay on Population* published; tax of ten per cent on incomes over £200 introduced
1799	Trade Unions suppressed; Napoleon appointed First Consul in France
1799–1801	Commercial boom
1801	Union with Ireland; first British Census
1802	Peace with France; Peel introduces first factory legislation
1803	War with France; General Enclosure Act simplifies process of enclosure of common land
1805	Battle of Trafalgar: Nelson defeats the French and Spanish fleets
1809–10	Commercial boom
1811	Depression because of Orders in Council; 'Luddite' disturbances in Nottinghamshire and Yorkshire; George, Prince of Wales, made Prince Regent
1813	East India Company's monopoly abolished
1815	Battle of Waterloo: defeat of Napoleon; peace in Europe: Congress of Vienna; Corn Law passed setting price of corn at 80s. per quarter
1815–17	Commercial boom
1817	Slump; the Blanketeers' march and other disturbances
1819	Peterloo massacre: troops intervene at mass reform meeting, killing 11 and wounding 400
1820	Death of George III; accession of George IV
1821–3	Famine in Ireland
1824	Commercial boom
1825	Trade Unions legalized; Stockton and Darlington railway opens; commercial depression
1829	Catholic Emancipation, ending most denials or restrictions of Catholic civil rights, ownership of property, and holding of public office
1830	Death of George IV; accession of William IV; Liverpool and Manchester railway opens
1830–2	First major cholera epidemic; Whigs in power under Grey
1831	'Swing' riots in rural areas against the mechanization of agriculture
1832	Great Reform Bill brings climax to period of political

reform, enlarging the franchise and restructuring
representation in Parliament

1833   Factory Act limits child labour; beginning of Oxford
Movement in Anglican Church

1834   Slavery abolished in the British Empire; parish
workhouses instituted; Robert Owen founds the
Grand National Consolidated Trade Union: action
by government against 'illegal oaths' in unionism
results in failure of GNCTU and transportation of
six 'Tolpuddle Martyrs'

1835   Municipal Reform Act extends local government
franchise to all ratepayers

1835–6   Commercial boom: 'little' railway mania

1837   Death of William IV; accession of Queen Victoria

1838   Anti-Corn Law League established; People's Charter
drafted

1839   Chartist riots

1840   Penny post instituted

1841   Tories in power: Peel ministry

1844   Bank Charter Act; Rochdale Co-operative Society
founded; Royal Commission on Health of Towns

1844–5   Railway mania: massive speculation and investment
leads to building of 5,000 miles of track; potato
famine begins in Ireland

1846   Corn Law abolished; Whigs in power

1848   Revolutions in Europe; Public Health Act

VOL. 5 THE MODERN AGE

1851   Great Exhibition

1852   Derby's first minority Conservative government

1852–5   Aberdeen's coalition government

1853   Gladstone's first budget

1854   Northcote–Trevelyan civil service report

1854–6   Crimean War, defending European interests in the
Middle East against Russia

1855   Palmerston's first government

1857–8   Second Opium War opens China to European trade

1858–9   Derby's second minority Conservative government

1858   Indian Mutiny and India Act

1859   Publication of Darwin's *Origin of Species*

1859–65	Palmerston's second Liberal government
1860	Anglo-French 'Cobden' treaty and Gladstone's budget codify and extend principles of free trade
1861	Death of Albert, Prince Consort
1862	Limited Liability Act provides vital stimulus to accumulation of capital in shares
1865	Death of Palmerston (October)
1865–6	Russell's second Liberal government
1866	Russell–Gladstone moderate Reform Bill fails
1866–8	Derby's third minority Conservative government
1867	Derby–Disraeli Reform Act; Dominion of Canada Act
1868	Disraeli succeeds Derby as Prime Minister (February)
1868–74	Gladstone's first Liberal government
1869	Suez Canal opened; Irish Church disestablished
1870	Irish Land Act; Forster–Ripon English Elementary Education Act; Married Women's Property Act extends the rights of women in marriage
1872	Scottish Education Act
1873	Gladstone government resigns after defeat on Irish Universities Bill; Disraeli declines to take office
1874–80	Disraeli's second Conservative government
1875	Disraeli buys Suez Canal shares, gaining a controlling interest for Britain
1875	Agricultural depression deepens
1875–6	R. A. Cross's Conservative social reforms passed
1876	Victoria proclaimed Empress of India; massacres of Christians in Turkish Bulgaria provoke anti-Turkish campaign in Britain, led by Gladstone
1877	Confederation of British and Boer states in South Africa
1878	Congress of Berlin; Disraeli announces 'peace with honour'
1879	Trade depression; Zulu War: British defeated at Isandhlwana, win at Ulundi
1879–80	Gladstone's Midlothian campaign denounces imperialism in Afghanistan and South Africa
1880–5	Gladstone's second Liberal government
1880–1	First Anglo-Boer War
1881	Irish Land and Coercion Acts

1882	Britain occupies Egypt; Triple Alliance between Germany, Austria, and Italy
1884–5	Reform and Redistribution Acts
1885	Death of Gordon at Khartoum; Burma annexed; Salisbury's first (minority) Conservative government
1886	Royal Niger Company chartered; gold found in Transvaal; Gladstone's third Liberal government introduces first Home Rule Bill for Ireland: Liberal Party splits
1886–92	Salisbury's second (Conservative–Liberal-Unionist) government
1887	British East Africa Company chartered
1888	County Councils Act establishes representative county authorities
1889	London dock strike; British South Africa Company chartered
1892–4	Gladstone's fourth (minority) Liberal government
1893	Second Home Rule Bill rejected by the Lords; Independent Labour Party founded
1894–5	Rosebery's minority Liberal government
1895–1902	Salisbury's third Unionist ministry
1896–8	Sudan conquered
1898	German naval expansion begins
1899–1902	Second Anglo-Boer War
1899	(autumn)British disasters in South Africa
1900	Khaki election won by Salisbury; formation of Labour Representation Committee; Commonwealth of Australia Act
1901	Death of Victoria; accession of Edward VII
1902	Balfour's Education Act; Anglo-Japanese alliance
1902–5	Balfour's Unionist government
1903	Chamberlain's Tariff Reform campaign starts
1904	Anglo-French *Entente*
1905–8	Campbell-Bannerman's Liberal government
1906	Liberals win general election (January); Labour Party formed
1907	Anglo-Russian *Entente*
1908–15	Asquith's Liberal government
1908	Asquith's Old Age Pensions plan introduced

1909	Churchill's Employment Exchanges introduced; Lloyd George's budget rejected by Lords; Union of South Africa Act
1910	(January) General election: Liberal government retains office
	(May) Death of Edward VII; accession of George V
	(December) General election: Liberal government again retains office
1911	Parliament Act curtails power of the House of Lords, establishes five-yearly elections; Lloyd George's National Insurance Act; Moroccan crisis
1911–12	Railway, mining, and coal strikes
1912	Anglo-German navy talks fail
1912–14	Third Home Rule Act (for Ireland) and Welsh Church Disestablishment Act passed, but suspended
1914	(28 June) Assassination of Archduke Ferdinand at Sarajevo
	(4 August) British Empire enters the First World War
1915–16	Dardanelles expedition, ending in British withdrawal from Gallipoli
1916	Battle of the Somme; battle of Jutland; Lloyd George succeeds Asquith as Prime Minister
1917	Battle of Passchendaele
1918	End of First World War (11 November); Lloyd George coalition government returned in 'coupon election' (December)
1919	Treaty of Versailles establishes peace in Europe
1921	Miners seek support of dockers' and railwaymen's unions (the 'Triple Alliance') in major strike: on 'Black Friday' the dockers and railwaymen back down, and the alliance is broken; Lloyd George concludes treaty with Sinn Fein
1922	Fall of Lloyd George; Bonar Law heads Conservative government
1923	Baldwin becomes Conservative Prime Minister; general election
1924	(January) MacDonald leads first Labour government
	(November) Conservatives return to office under Baldwin

1925	Britain goes back on the gold standard
1926	General Strike (3–12 May)
1929	General election; MacDonald leads second Labour government
1931	Financial crisis and run on the pound; Britain abandons the gold standard; MacDonald resigns and is returned in the election to head National government
1932	Ottawa Conference on imperial trade institutes protective tarriffs
1935	Conservatives win general election: Baldwin succeeds MacDonald as Prime Minister; Hoare–Laval pact on Abyssinia; Government of India Act
1936	Death of King George V; abdication of Edward VIII: George VI becomes king
1937	Neville Chamberlain succeeds Baldwin as Conservative Prime Minister
1938	Chamberlain meets Hitler at Berchtesgaden, Godesberg, and Munich
1939	British guarantee to Poland; British Empire declares war on Germany (3 September)
1940	Churchill succeeds Chamberlain as Prime Minister; withdrawal from Dunkirk; Battle of Britain
1941	*Luftwaffe* 'blitz' on many British cities; Soviet Union and United States enter the war
1942	Loss of Singapore; Montgomery's victory at El Alamein; battle of Stalingrad; Beveridge Report on social security
1943	Successful campaign in North Africa; Anglo-American armies invade Italy
1944	D-day invasion of France; Butler's Education Act
1945	End of war in Europe (8 May) and in far East (15 August); general election: massive Labour victory and Attlee becomes Prime Minister
1947	Coal and other industries nationalized; convertibility crisis; transfer of power to independent India, Pakistan, and Burma
1949	NATO founded; devaluation of the pound by Cripps
1950	General election: Labour retains power by narrow

majority; outbreak of war in Korea

1951	Festival of Britain; general election: Conservatives defeat Labour, and Churchill again becomes Prime Minister
1952	Death of King George VI; Queen Elizabeth II proclaimed
1954	British troops withdraw from Egypt
1955	Eden becomes Prime Minister; general election won by Conservatives
1956	Anglo-French invasion of Suez, followed by withdrawal
1957	Eden resigns; Macmillan becomes Prime Minister
1959	General election: Conservatives win with larger majority
1963	French veto Britain's application to join the European Common Market; test-ban treaty in Moscow limits nuclear testing; Douglas-Home succeeds Macmillan as Prime Minister
1964	General election: Labour under Harold Wilson win narrow majority
1966	General election: Labour win with much larger majority
1967	Devaluation of the pound
1970	General election: Conservatives under Edward Heath returned to office
1972	National miners' strike; Stormont government abolished in Northern Ireland
1973	Britain enters European Common Market
1974	National miners' strike; two general elections: Labour under Harold Wilson win both with narrow majorities
1975	Popular referendum confirms British membership of the Common Market
1976	Economic crisis: Britain obtains help from International Monetary Fund
1979	Devolution referendums in Wales and Scotland; general election: Conservatives under Mrs Thatcher returned to office; independence granted to Zimbabwe (Rhodesia)
1980	Britain becomes self-sufficient in North Sea oil

1981	Social Democratic Party founded
1982	Britain defeats Argentina in war over the Falkland Islands
1983	General election: Mrs Thatcher's Conservative government returned with massive majority; Cruise missiles installed
1984	Miners' strike
1985	Miners' strike ends after a year; Anglo-Irish Hillsborough Agreement signed
1986	Channel Tunnel treaty signed; 'Big Bang' in Stock Exchange
1987	General election: Mrs Thatcher's Conservative government again returned with a majority of over 100; Stock Exchange collapse in the autumn
1989	Poll tax introduced
1990	Resignation of Mrs Thatcher; John Major becomes Prime Minister
1991	Gulf War against Iraq

STUARTS AND HANOVERIANS
1603–1837

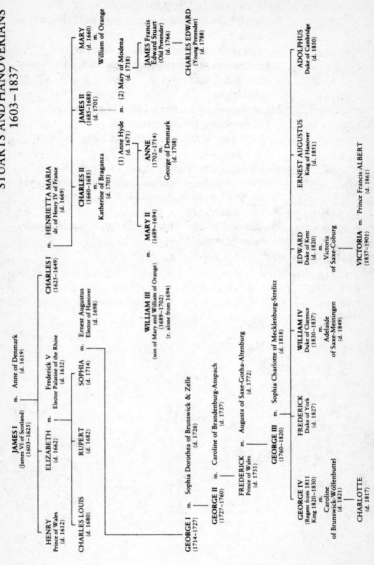

PRIME MINISTERS 1721–1851

Sir Robert Walpole	Apr. 1721	Henry Addington	Mar. 1801
Earl of Wilmington	Feb. 1741	William Pitt	May 1804
Henry Pelham	Aug. 1743	William Wyndham	
Duke of Newcastle	Mar. 1754	Grenville	Feb. 1806
Duke of Devonshire	Nov. 1756	Duke of Portland	Mar. 1807
Duke of Newcastle	July 1757	Spencer Perceval	Oct. 1809
Earl of Bute	May 1762	Earl of Liverpool	June 1812
George Grenville	Apr. 1763	George Canning	Apr. 1827
Marquess of		Viscount Goderich	Aug. 1827
Rockingham	July 1765	Duke of Wellington	Jan. 1828
Earl of Chatham	July 1766	Earl Grey	Nov. 1830
Duke of Grafton	Oct. 1768	Viscount Melbourne	July 1834
Lord North	Jan. 1770	Duke of Wellington	Nov. 1834
Marquess of		Sir Robert Peel	Dec. 1834
Rockingham	Mar. 1782	Viscount Melbourne	Apr. 1835
Earl of Shelburne	July 1782	Sir Robert Peel	Aug. 1841
Duke of Portland	Apr. 1783	Lord John Russell	June 1846
William Pitt	Dec. 1783